KANATA

KANATA

An Anthology of Canadian
Children's Literature

Editors
Mary Rubio / Glenys Stow

Consultant
Ken Haycock

Methuen   Toronto • London • Sydney • Wellington

Copyright © 1976 by Methuen Publications
(A division of the Carswell Company Limited)

ISBN 0-458-91320-0
    0-458-91380-4

Designed by Michael van Elsen

Printed and bound in Canada
79 78 77 76 1 2 3 4 5 6

Canadian Cataloguing in Publication Data

Main entry under title:

Kanata

ISBN 0-458-91380-4 bd.   ISBN 0-458-91320-0 pa.

1. Children's literature, Canadian (English).*
I. Rubio, Mary, 1939-   II. Stow, Glenys, 1931-

PS8233.K35   j C810'.8'09282   C76-017047-9
PR9194.4.K35

To the children of Canada,
especially Belinda, Mark, Veda,
Arthur, Donald, Tracy and Jennifer.

Contents

In the Beginning

Voices in the Wilderness

Mosaic

Acknowledgements

We are indebted to Dr. Elizabeth Waterston for providing us with the initial encouragement for this project; to Sarah Swartz and to Sandra Esche for editorial assistance; to Judith St. John, Margaret Maloney, Dana Tenny, and Milada Dufek of the Osborne Collection of Early Children's Books and to Marian Cooke and Doris Scott of Boys and Girls House in Toronto, to Lois Fleming of the Kitchener Public Library, and to the University of Guelph for making our initial research possible; to Ken Haycock, Isla Key, Jean Stevens, Bruce Munro, and Beverly Matson, and other educators across Canada whose advice helped us shape our materials; to Margaret Laurence who looked over our proposed table of contents and offered suggestions; and, most of all, to our husbands, who have been patient and encouraging.

Glenys Stow
Mary Rubio

Kanata

Why do we call our country Canada? Where did the name come from?

Some people say that when Spanish explorers sailed into Chaleur Bay on the Maritime coast they took one look at the rocky cliffs and said "Aca nada", meaning "There is nothing here". Some of the first white settlers who followed also thought that this was an empty land. As they looked around them at the tangled forests, they imagined that no happy people had ever lived here.

But they were wrong. The first Canadians had come from Asia, across a land bridge over the Bering Strait, twenty-five thousand years before. All across the land they settled in their tribal communities, taking their food and clothing from the wilderness around them. On long winter nights they told stories about the gods and animal spirits who loved and guided them. They spoke of how the world began, how their people had been given the necessities of life such as fire and corn, and how their warriors had done brave or foolish deeds. In 1534 Jacques Cartier wrote about his exploration of this country and of the native communities he encountered. He called this new land *Kanata* (Kah-nah-tah), which is an Indian word meaning "village" or "community".

When the first settlers came, they formed new communities in the wilderness, and they too told stories—stories they remembered from the old country. But soon they began to invent new tales which belonged to Canada. In Quebec, the settlers told tall tales about mysterious animals or ghostly and fearsome happenings. In the Maritimes, people told the old stories and sang the old songs; but they added new ones about giant loggers and wily fishermen. In Upper Canada, English-speaking settlers created story characters who battled with fire, winter, and loneliness. On the prairies the best way to deal with the rain which dripped through the sod roof was to joke and sing about it. And in the west the old passion for tales of adventure was still awake among those who crossed the desolate mountains in search of gold.

So we have called our anthology of these stories, songs and verses *Kanata*, and we hope that reading them will help you see how many different people, from many times and places, have made this land into their community.

Life in Canada today is very different from what it was in native times or in settler days. Many of us live in cities. World events like wars or industrial advances change our lives and our beliefs. But some of the things which were important to the people who lived here before us still matter to us now. We still love animals; we still escape to the wild country when we can; we still want to learn how to do certain things well and how to stand on our own feet; and we all need to belong—in our family, with our friends, and in our own special place. Writers today describe modern life, but they still speak about many of the truths which the old story-tellers knew.

All of our different people, and all of our special times and places, join together to make a many-coloured mosaic pattern. You and I are part of that pattern, as are all the people who have told or written the stories and poems in this book. Canada is not a place where there is nothing; it is our village, our community, our *kanata*.

In the Beginning

How Raven Created the World

by Ronald Melzack

In the beginning, there was only Raven and the falling snowflakes.

Raven sailed through the soft silvery glow of the universe which stretched endlessly around him. Sparkling snowflakes swirled past him and tumbled around in circles as his wings swayed ever so slightly.

Once, Raven caught some snowflakes on his outstretched wings. He lowered one wing, and the snowflakes trickled down to his wingtip and made a little snowball. He amused himself as he flew, gently lowering and raising his wing, and watched the little snowball grow as it rolled back and forth. Then, with a great sweep of his wing, he hurled the snowball through the air.

Raven watched, fascinated, as his snowball soared across the sky, picking up more snowflakes as it hurtled along. It grew larger and larger until it was immense. Raven flew after it, sailed above it, and then lowered himself gently onto it. He stretched out his legs and realized that he had never before stood on solid ground. He had been flying for as long as he could remember, and it felt good to rest his wings.

Raven felt an itch near his beak. He scratched it and, to his astonishment, his beak moved! He pushed it up so that it sat on his forehead. His wings felt strange, and, as he moved them, his wing-cape slipped off his shoulders. He stood upright on two legs and moved his hands slowly over his face. He felt his eyes, his nose, his mouth. His fingers examined the beak on his forehead.

The soft, white snow-hills sparkled in the pale, silvery light. Raven kicked away at the snow with his foot, and soon he saw rich brown clay. He picked up the clay and moulded little seeds out of it. Then Raven swept his wing-cape across his shoulders, lowered his beak, and flew from place to place and planted the seeds. Wherever he planted them a forest grew up—tree after tree, with herbs and plants around their roots. Raven thought this new land was beautiful and he called it Earth. The place he came from he called the Sky.

Raven liked Earth and each day he flew to see all the things he had created. He wandered through the forests and tended the plants and flowers, especially the tiny shoots that sprang out of the earth and grew slowly upward.

One plant grew quickly, so quickly that Raven could actually see it grow. Leaves sprouted out of the plant, and little buds near the leaves grew into pea-pods.

As he watched, he saw a pea-pod move and jiggle, yet there was no wind. It shook and quivered and then it split open, and a little living creature popped out. It jumped around and kicked the snow. The creature was cold, and, as it jumped up and down, its teeth chattered.

Raven went up to the newcomer and smiled. "Who are you?" he asked.

"I came from that pod," said the creature. "I was tired of lying there, so I kicked out a hole and jumped through!"

Raven laughed heartily. "You're a funny fellow! You look a little familiar, though I've never seen you before!" And he laughed again. "I created that pod plant myself, but I had no idea that you would jump out."

"And where did *you* come from?" asked the little creature.

"I have always been here," said Raven. "Come to think of it, you look a lot like me, except that you don't have a beak on your forehead. I will call you Man and I will be your friend." Raven plucked feathers from his wing-cape and made a little parka for Man to wear and keep his body warm.

That was how the first man was created, and Raven watched many more men, and women too, hop out of the pea-pod plant.

Raven fed the people with berries from the plants that he had grown. But the people needed more food. And so Raven made the animals and he made them of clay. After he had fashioned them in the shapes that delighted him, he set the clay creatures out to dry in the cool air. And when they had dried out, Raven called the people to behold what he had made. The people thought they were beautiful. Then Raven told the people to close their eyes. He pulled his beak down over his mouth, and waved his wings five times over the shapes. Soon they started to breathe and move. They were alive. Raven raised his mask and told the people to look. When they saw the animals moving, full of life, they cried out with pleasure. Raven experimented with these creatures until they looked just right to him. And that is how he learned to make every kind of animal, fish, and bird, and he taught each kind to live on the earth, in the sea, or in the air.

Raven showed the animals to the people and said that some animals would be their food as soon as people learned to hunt. But that would not be easy, because the pale, silvery glow of the sky was just enough for people to see things close at hand. When men wanted to walk to distant places, they had to grope about with their hands and find things out by listening.

Men heard the howling of the wolves, the grunting of the bears, and the growling of the foxes. In the sea the seals snorted, the walruses wheezed, the whales blew. Birds whistled and sang, insects hummed. Men heard, too, the whispering of the winds, the rustle and murmur of the leaves, and the surging of the surf against the shore.

Raven loved all the creatures he had created, but there were none that he respected or admired more than the sparrows. One day, he called a little sparrow and said to her, "Far off in the universe lies the source of all light. Even though you are small and plain, you are the hardiest and bravest creature of all. Therefore I command you to fly out into the universe and bring back Light so

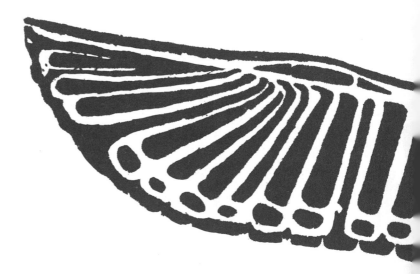

that people may see the world, the animals, and one another."

The little sparrow flew off and stayed away in the darkness until Raven thought she would never come back. At last, he heard the whirr of her wings and felt her floating down and settling on his hand. The sparrow carried three little packets in her beak, each wrapped in a leaf. She gave them to Raven.

Raven opened one of the leaves and saw a ball of brilliant, dazzling gold. He called it the Sun. He threw it into the air, and immediately a great radiance filled the earth and dazzled everyone.

For the first time, people could see the earth on which they lived. They saw the woods, the animals on land and in the sea, and the birds in the air. They rejoiced at all the beauty around them. Life became a new and greater thing for all of them. When the sun set, Raven opened another leaf, and in it was a ball of iron. Raven threw it up into the air and called it the Moon. Raven called the light of the sun Day and the light of the moon Night, and both the sun and the moon have gracefully shared the sky with each other ever since.

Now people were happy. Raven taught them to build igloos and tents to shelter themselves from the wind and the storms. He taught them to make kayaks and big boats so that they could sail on the sea and hunt the sea-creatures. He taught them to make spears and other weapons to hunt the animals that roam the land. And he showed them how to build a fire to warm themselves when they were cold, and to cook the meat when it was too tough to eat.

Men and animals flourished on earth and their numbers kept increasing. But the land was too small to hold them all. One day, Raven said to the people, "So that there may be food and space enough for all, the old must henceforth make way for the young." And for the first time, the oldest of all living things—people and animals, plants and trees—weakened and died. Yet men and animals continued to flourish, and their numbers kept increasing.

One day, Raven moulded clay to make new kinds of animals for his people. The clay was too wet, and when he set it out to dry, it all ran together and made a huge serpent unlike any other animal. The serpent slithered down to the sea, and swam around near shore, waiting to pounce on the men in their boats. Men rode up to it in their kayaks and tried to harpoon it, but all the harpoons bounced off its sides.

Raven saw the hopeless struggle and said to the little sparrow, who followed him everywhere, "Fly out and hover above the serpent while I hunt it from my kayak." Then Raven followed the sparrow to the serpent.

The sparrow glided above the serpent and inspected it intently. Soon she pointed to its soft belly, and Raven threw his harpoon. The serpent exploded with a tremendous roar. The men shouted with joy as they watched bits of serpent fly up into the air and then come crashing down into the sea, where they turned into islands. Land shot up near land, and the whole became a wide and spacious coast. In this way, new land was created and there was enough room on earth for everybody, men and animals too.

One day, just after the sun had gone down and the sky was a deep, rich blue, Raven gathered all the people and said to them, "I am your Creator. To me you owe your lives and your land, and you must never forget me."

Raven drew his beak down over his mouth and swept his wing-cape across his shoulders. He spread his wings wide and sailed up to the sky, where it was dark. In one wing he held the last of the leaves that the sparrow had given him. He shook open the leaf, and in it were little pieces of silver. He threw the silver pieces into the air, and they scattered across the whole sky. Raven called them the Stars. The people were enchanted by the tiny, glittering lights, and they sang out in awe and delight.

And this was the way Raven made the earth, the men, and the animals, and the sun, the moon, and the stars.

Morning Mood
by M. Panegoosho

I wake with morning yawning in my mouth,
With laughter, see a teakettle spout steaming.
I wake with hunger in my belly
And I lie still, so beautiful it is, it leaves me dazed,
The timelessness of the light.

Grandma cares for me, and our family needs nothing more.
They share each other for pleasure
As mother knows, who learns of happiness
From her own actions
They did not even try to be beautiful, only true,
But beauty is here, it is a custom.

This place of unbroken joy,
Giving out its light today—only today—not tomorrow.

Kajortoq and the Crow

by Maurice Metayer

Kajortoq, the red fox, was strolling along the edge of a cliff when she chanced to see a moose grazing on some moss. Approaching the moose Kajortoq said, "I know of a place near here where there is wild fruit. It is on a narrow ledge of rocks which we can reach by following the path halfway up the cliff."

The moose followed Kajortoq without hesitation and, jumping over rock hollows, soon found himself in a precarious position on the edge of the precipice. The fox, who had moved ahead of the moose, turned and warned, "Be careful here. It is easy to lose your footing. Take care not to fall. Jump quickly to this side!" The moose did as Kajortoq directed but when his hooves landed on the slippery rocks they struck a loose stone and he fell to the bottom of the cliff. When Kajortoq reached the bottom she found the moose dead and proceeded to make a meal of her victim.

Days later she had finished all of the meat and set out to continue her hunting. Eventually she spotted a bird sitting on its eggs in a nest at the top of a tree. She called up to the bird, "I want to eat some eggs. Throw one to me!" Although the bird valued her eggs, she was frightened and allowed one of them to fall to the ground. Kajortoq ate it quickly and moved away from the tree.

Soon she was back demanding more eggs. This time the bird replied, "No, I will not give them to you." At this Kajortoq screamed, "If you don't give me some of your eggs I will take them all for I shall cut down this tree with my axe!" Intimidated, the poor bird let a few more eggs fall to the ground and the fox ate her fill and moved on.

Tulugaq, the crow, had been watching these events and now he came to speak to the bird. "Why did you let that renegade fox eat your eggs?" he asked. The bird explained that if she hadn't given Kajortoq a few of the eggs she would have used her axe to cut down the tree and all the eggs would have been lost. Tulugaq replied, "That fox is nothing but a liar; she has no axe! She is only trying to frighten you."

When the crow had gone, it was not long before Kajortoq returned demanding still more eggs and threatening once more to cut down the tree. This time the bird spoke without fear or hesitation.

"I will give you no more eggs. I am keeping them for myself."

Kajortog was suspicious. "Who has been telling tales about me?"

"The big crow told me that you have no axe and cannot cut down this tree where I have my nest," replied the bird. "I shall give you no more eggs!"

The red fox moved off muttering, "That crow is nothing but a chatter box." She headed toward an open field where she lay down, pretending to be dead. Curious, Tulugaq approached the fox's still form, cawing noisily and pecking at her buttocks and hind feet with his beak to see if the fox would stir. With great difficulty the fox remained perfectly still until Tulugaq, certain that Kajortoq was dead, moved toward her head in order to peck out her eyes. Suddenly the crow found himself imprisoned in the fox's strong jaws.

Kajortoq carried her victim to a small hill and prepared to eat him. However, before she could begin her meal, the crow spoke.

"Where is the wind coming from?" the crow asked.

The fox thought, "Are you crazy to ask such a question?"

She opened her mouth wide to say so and the crow flew away.

Glorious It Is
a Copper Eskimo poem

Glorious it is to see
The caribou flocking down from the forests
And beginning
Their wanderings to the north.
Timidly they watch
For the pitfalls of man.
Glorious it is to see
The great herds from the forests
Spreading out over plains of white.
Glorious to see.

Glorious it is to see
Early summer's short-haired caribou
Beginning to wander.
Glorious to see them trot
To and fro
Across the promontories,
Seeking a crossing place.

Glorious it is
To see the great musk oxen
Gathering in herds.
The little dogs they watch for
When they gather in herds.
Glorious to see.

Glorious it is
To see young women
Gathering in little groups
And paying visits in the houses—
Then all at once the men
Do so want to be manly,
While the girls simply
Think of some little lie.

Glorious it is
To see long-haired winter caribou
Returning to the forests.
Fearfully they watch
For the little people,
While the herd follows the ebb-mark of the sea
With a storm of clattering hooves.
Glorious it is
When wandering time is come.

"Across the Mountains"

from *Akavak* by James Houston

Akavak's grandfather has set out over the wild mountain ranges to see his brother for the last time before he dies. Akavak goes with him, and the two save each other from death more than once before they reach their jouney's end.

When Akavak left the snowhouse in the morning, he saw long, thin white clouds flaring across the sky. These were driven by high winds far above them. His grandfather looked at them but said nothing. Akavak watched him hurrying to harness the tired, half-starving dogs.

They pushed forward once more, finding that the air was thin and hard to breathe. Akavak was so hungry that he sometimes lost all sense of time and seemed to float beside the sled.

He had been climbing in this trance for some while when he noticed that his grandfather was no longer beside the sled. Looking back down the trail, he saw him sitting hunched in the snow, his head on his knees.

Akavak halted the dogs and hurried back to help him.

"Go on. Go on," said the old man in a slow, thin voice. "I will rest here a while and then follow you to the top."

"No, Grandfather. You will come with me now. We must stay together," Akavak said with determination.

Akavak helped his grandfather up and supported him to the sled. Then he wrapped a caribou sleeping skin around his shoulders. The old man lay half on the sled but managed somehow to push with his feet, and in this way they started upward again. Akavak shouted at the dogs and beat on the wooden runners to frighten them, and they crept steadily forward.

Finally he could see the top, but he did not dare to rest in their slow passage upward, for the sky was darkening and clouds now hid the high peaks. The wind rushed in from the southwest, howling as it struck the frozen mountains.

Soon they were climbing the last rise, and then they suddenly stopped and stared. The wide glacier lay before them, grey and ancient, laced with new white snow. Beyond it stretched the great flat plain of the high plateau, in places blown entirely clear by the violent winds, so that huge patches of tundra and many stones shaped like skulls were exposed to sight.

The dogs lay down, and the travellers turned the sled onto its side, against the rising wind. They, too, lay down, waiting for their strength to return to them.

"Come," said the grandfather. "We must cross the glacier there at the narrow place. Beyond it we will build a snowhouse."

Slowly they followed the dogs, stumbling across the blinding whiteness of the glacier. Once they heard it creak and moan beneath their feet.

"I do not like this place," said Akavak's grandfather, and he slid the harpoon out from under the sled's lashings. He started to walk forward, feeling carefully before him with the bone chisel. But for once his keen instinct for danger warned him too late.

With an awesome "swoosh," the snow around Akavak

collapsed and fell into a great yawning blue abyss. He watched with horror as the scrambling, howling dogs disappeared. Then, as though by evil magic, the sled beside him slipped away, and he could not longer see his grandfather. In the swirling snow, Akavak's foot caught on something as he started to plunge into the awful abyss. Half turning, flailing, gripping, he lost his mitts and felt his bare hands strike something solid. It was the edge of the ice wall. He held on for his life. The thunder below him died away, and everything was silent again.

His muscles ached with deadly weariness, and his bare hands grew numb against the ice. But still he waited, his eyes closed, holding on to life with his fingertips. How long before he, too, must fall?

He did not see the rough old hand reach over the edge of the abyss, but he felt it grasp him by the hood of his parka, and another hand took his wrist. A rasping voice called, "Kojo! Kojo!" and in another moment he felt a sealskin line lashed around his wrist.

The old man called, "Ush, ush," to the dog. Then Akavak felt his hood jerk upward, and his arm was nearly pulled from its socket as he was drawn up out of the gaping hole in the glacier.

The boy and the old man lay beside the open crevasse, too exhausted to move. Kojo, the starving dog that looked like a wolf, stood over them, with the dog line still attached to Akavak's wrist. For a moment it looked as though Kojo was the hunter and these creatures stretched on the snow were his prey.

Akavak's hands were white and would not bend. His grandfather held them under his own parka, against the warmth of his body until they burned like fire and the fingers could move once more. Then, because Akavak had no mitts, he drew his hands up into the long fur sleeves of his parka.

The sled and all the dogs were gone save Kojo. Akavak could scarcely believe the swiftness of death that had taken Nowjah, Pasti, and the others and buried them deep in the glacier forever.

18

The three staggered away from the awful blue hole and fearfully crossed the remaining tongue of the glacier. When they reached solid ground once more, they felt on their faces stinging grains of icy snow that blew down from the surrounding peaks. Slowly they made their way toward a small gully on the high plateau. It would give them some protection from the mighty force of the rising wind. They shambled on, the old man holding Kojo's broken harness for support. Akavak tried not to think of what they would do now. They had no food. Without dogs or sled, there could be no going back or forward from this frightening place.

Akavak saw it first, half buried in the snow. It was so old and frozen that the dog did not even smell it. Two great horns curved upward, and one empty eye socket stared at them from the whitened skull.

"Umingmuk," said his grandfather, "musk ox, long dead, killed by wolves perhaps."

"Nothing left," said Akavak sadly, kicking away the snow from the bare bones that lay scattered like grey driftwood among the useless tufts of long hair.

Bending over to examine it, the old man said, "That is a piece of skin, strong heavy skin," and he pried the end of a large stiff piece away from the frozen ground. Reaching into his hunting bag, he drew out a small knife and gave it to Akavak, together with one of his mitts.

"Cut away as large a piece as you can," he said. Then the old man stamped hard on the bleached skull, and the two big horns broke away.

"Bring these also," he said, and without another word he limped away toward the rocky cliff at the end of the little gully. In the wind, the caribou sleeping skin that was still wrapped around his hunched shoulders flapped like the wings of some ancient bird.

Akavak watched his grandfather as he edged along, carefully studying the cliff face, sometimes taking off his mitt to feel it. Then suddenly he dropped to his knees and started scraping and digging in a frenzied way. Akavak wondered if the time had come, as his father had warned, when his grandfather's spirit might wander away from him and he must take care of him.

With the knife, Akavak went on hacking and pulling at the useless frozen skin, looking at the gaping holes in it, knowing that it could have no warmth. With a jerk, he pulled free a large piece of the hide and straightened up.

He saw his grandfather walking slowly toward him. In his hands he held four stones. Wearily the old man chose a site and waved to Akavak to put the frozen hide down on the snow and place the stones on top. From his hunting bag, he drew a thin ivory blade and licked it until it was covered with a thin coating of ice and could be used to cut the heavy snow blocks. Together they worked and built a small strong igloo to stand against the forces of the mountain winds.

Once inside, Akavak's grandfather cleaned the snow out of a hollow in the largest stone and, taking a small pouch from his hunting bag, removed some frozen seal fat. He held a piece of this in his mouth to soften it. Next he cut a small piece off his inner clothing to serve as a wick, and then he whirled his bow drill in its wooden socket until the dry wood shavings smouldered and burned. Carefully he lit the oil-soaked wick, and it sputtered and burst into flame, casting a small warm glow inside the sparkling white of the new snow walls.

They placed the frozen musk-ox skin on the soft snow floor, and over this they spread the caribou skin the old man had worn around his shoulders. They lay down with Kojo between them, using the dog's body heat to keep them from freezing.

That night, the terrible wind screamed and thundered over their small igloo, trying to tear it from the high plateau and fling it down the mountains. But their house was strong and round and carefully trimmed, with no corners for the wind to grasp, and as Akavak drew his head deep into his hood and hugged his arms next to his body inside his parka, he thought, "I am alive, and my grandfather

21

is alive, and together we shall cross this high plateau and see the land of my great uncle that lies beyond these mountains." He said that to himself, again and again, until he drifted off to sleep. He dreamed of clever Nowyah, and Pasti the strong one, and the three young dogs lost to him forever.

When Akavak awoke, he heard the sharp click of stone against stone. He rolled over and saw his grandfather hunched beside the light, holding a flat stone in his hand. His grandfather judged the angle, then carefully struck the stone a sharp blow, causing a chip to fly off. Again and again he struck the flint, each time examining the shape. Gradually, as the day wore on, the stone was formed into a sharp blade, almost as long as Akavak's hand.

On the following day, the wind continued to thunder against the house. Akavak and his grandfather chewed pieces of skin cut from their boot tops to ease their terrible hunger, but always the old man went on grinding and sharpening the chipped blade.

They slept again, and so dark and terrible was the storm around their house that they could not tell if it were night or day.

When they awoke, Akavak's grandfather said, "When I slept, I dreamed." As he spoke, he trimmed the dying lamp wick and squinted his old eyes into the flame. "I dreamed that I walked up along the shining path of the moon and flew among the stars. I could see all the mountains and the rivers and the sea beneath me. Great herds of caribou I saw, and mighty whales rolling in the sea, and huge flights of geese. Seeing these things seemed to ease my hunger. I was pleased to have such a night journey, but when I grew tired, I found that I did not have the power to return to the earth. I felt a great sadness, for I knew I would not see my son or my grandson again, or my brother who lives beyond this mountain, or his sons. My mind was full of grief that I had not visited them. That was all that I minded about leaving this earth.

"And when I awoke just now, I thought again and again that I am an old man and may never reach my brother's land, and my hand shall not touch his hand again."

Akavak could not answer his grandfather, but he knew that what he said was very important to him.

With the new stone blade, the old man showed his grandson how to shape and polish the musk-ox horns. Akavak then scraped out the hollow insides until they were smooth. When they were finished, he filled the new cups with snow scraped from the inside walls of the igloo and held them above the lamp until the snow melted and turned to water. As Akavak held the cups over the flame of the lamp, he thought that although the great storm held them like prisoners in the little house, he and his grandfather were always busy when they were awake, working to stay alive. They were determined to leave the mountain.

The Giant Bear
by Kiakshuk

There once was a giant bear
who followed people for his prey.
He was so big he swallowed them whole:
Then they smothered to death inside him
if they hadn't already died of fright.

Either the bear attacked them on the run,
or if they crawled into a cave
where he could not squeeze his enormous body in,
he stabbed them with his whiskers like toothpicks,
drawing them out one by one,
and gulped them down.

No one knew what to do
until a wise man went out and let the bear swallow him,
sliding right down his throat into the big, dark, hot, slimy
    stomach.
And once inside there, he took his knife
and simply cut him open,
killing him of course.

He carved a door in the bear's belly
and threw out those who had been eaten before,
and then he stepped out himself
and went home to get help with the butchering.

Everyone lived on bear meat for a long time.
That's the way it goes:
Monster one minute, food the next.

The Rabbit Makes a Match

by Kay Hill

Ableegumooch the rabbit is a sociable creature, a little boastful perhaps, but kindhearted. So, when he saw his friend Keoonik the otter looking miserable, he wanted to know at once what was the matter and was there anything he could do. Well, it turned out that what the otter wanted was to get married. He wanted to marry Nesoowa, the daughter of Pipsolk; and the girl-otter was willing, but her father was not.

"Why not?" asked the rabbit, eying his friend. "You may not be the handsomest fellow in the world, Keoonik (otters can't compare with rabbits in looks), or the smartest (the rabbits are that), but you're honest and good-tempered and I dare say you'd provide quite a good living for a wife. Did you try anointing Pipsolk's head with bear grease?" This was the Indian way of asking if Keoonik had tried flattery on the girl's father.

"It wasn't any good," said Keoonik. "He thinks so well of himself already, nothing I could say would please him."

"How about a gift to sweeten his opinion?"

26

"No good. It isn't meat or presents he cares for—it's breeding and ancestors, and I haven't got any according to him." Keoonik added glumly—"I'm just an ordinary everyday kind of otter, not good enough for his daughter."

"Ah, Keoonik," signed the rabbit, "there are many like Pipsolk, full of silly pride. (Pride—that's one thing rabbits haven't!) Look, my friend, since I am known everywhere as the wittiest and most persuasive Wabanaki in Glooscap's world, wouldn't you like me to have a talk with Pipsolk?"

"What sort of talk?" asked Keoonik.

"I could tell him what a good fellow you really are and how much better it would be to have a decent son-in-law with no relatives than a bad one with too many!"

"Tell him I'm very fond of Nesoowa, and would try to make her happy."

"I'll tell him," said the rabbit, and off he went.

Ableegumooch found Pipsolk and his numerous family sliding happily down a muddy slope near their home on the lake. This is a favourite pastime of otters.

"Step over here, will you, Pipsolk," called the rabbit from a drier spot up the bank. "I'd like to talk with you about Nesoowa."

Pipsolk excused himself to his family and stepped over. "What about Nesoowa?"

"Isn't it time she was married?" queried Ableegumooch, "to a kind and hard-working husband? I don't know if it's occurred to you, but good husbands don't grow on blueberry bushes. And remember, with Nesoowa off your hands, you will have fewer mouths to feed."

"Very true," agreed Pipsolk, "but a man must do the best he can for his daughter. What kind of father would I be if I passed her over to the first common sort who came along? Tell me, Ableegumooch, who were your people?"

"Eh?"

"Your ancestors. Were they important? Were they well-bred?"

The rabbit stuck out his chest.

"Pipsolk," he said complacently, "my family is one of the best. I have a long and noble ancestry, with notables on every branch of the family tree since the days before the light of the sun."

"H'mm," Pipsolk nodded thoughtfully. "Can you show proof of your aristocratic background?"

"Certainly. Haven't you noticed how I always wear white in the winter time? That's the fashion of the aristocracy."

"Really? I didn't know that. But what about your split lip, Ableegumooch? It doesn't indicate anything common, does it?"

"On the contrary, it's a sign of breeding. In my circles, we always eat with knives, which is the polite way of feeding. One day my knife slipped, which is how my lip was damaged."

"But why is it your mouth and your whiskers keep moving even when you're still? Is that high style too?"

"Of course. You see, it's because I'm always meditating and planning great affairs. I talk to myself rather than to anyone of lesser quality. That's the way we gentlemen are!"

"I see. One more question. Why do you always hop? Why don't you walk like other people?"

"All my aristocratic forebears had a gait of their own," the rabbit explained loftily. "We gentle folk don't run like the vulgar."

"I'd no idea you were so well-bred, Ableegumooch," said Pipsolk. "Very well. You may have her."

The rabbit had opened his mouth to say something more about his aristocratic forebears, but now he closed it.

"I don't as a rule approve of marrying outside the tribe, but circumstances alter cases. Welcome, son-in-law."

Ableegumooch felt as though he had accidentally walked under an icy waterfall. He—to be married—and to an otter girl! The rabbit had never even thought of getting married! He opened his lips to say so, and hesitated, his whiskers twitching. Pipsolk was a man one didn't offend if one could help it. Many of his kind had a short way with rabbits! Moreover, the thought of marriage was rather pleasant, once one began to think about it. A pretty girl adds a nice touch to a wigwam. Besides, his grandmother was getting old and would be glad of help in the lodge.

He thought briefly of Keoonik, and worded an explanation silently in his mind. "I'm sorry, friend, but I didn't plan it this way, you know. I don't see how I can get out of it. Can I help it if Nesoowa's father wants the best for his daughter? You'll understand, I'm sure."

That night, Pipsolk invited all his relatives and friends to a feast and announced the engagement of Nesoowa to the well-known and aristocratic Ableegumooch, the marriage to take place at the end of the usual probationary period. It was customary among the Wabanaki of that time for a young man to provide for the family of his future bride for one year to show that he was capable of getting food and necessities for a wife and family. Keoonik was of course among the guests and, hearing the dreadful news, he could hardly believe his ears. He gave his faithless friend a long, bitter look as he left the party, and it quite shrivelled Ableegumooch for the moment.

The rabbit tried to find excuses for himself. "It wasn't my fault. It's too late now, anyway, to back down."

So he set up a lodge near Pipsolk's and brought over his grandmother, who complained bitterly at having to move to such a damp place near all those noisy otters, but the rabbit paid no attention. His mind was wholly occupied with the problem of feeding those otters. He knew it would be different from feeding himself and his grandmother. Rabbits live in meadows and forest undergrowth and are satisfied with herbs and grasses and tender twigs. Otters, on the other hand, live in or near water and like fish and frogs and salamanders for dinner. If Ableegumooch was to keep those otters fed, he must learn to be at home in the water, and a rabbit is not the best in the world when it comes to swimming. In fact, to be plain about it, of all swimmers and divers the rabbit is the very worst.

"Can you swim?" asked the young otters, with interest.

"Well—not yet," said Ableegumooch, adding cheerfully, "but I can learn." Ableegumooch was always willing to try.

He put his nose to the water. It smelled dank and weedy, not at all nice. He dipped one toe in the water to test its temperature— ugh, cold! He pulled his toe out again. After a good deal of sighing and dipping in and dipping out, the rabbit finally got himself into the water chest-deep and began to move his front paws in an awkward swimming motion. The watching otters nudged each other and chuckled. Then the rabbit tried to let go with his back feet, but sank at once and had to scramble in a panic to find solid ground again.

Nevertheless he kept trying, and after a whole day of failing and trying again, he managed to move a few strokes from shore, and all the otters applauded. Ableegumooch felt quite proud of himself, though he couldn't understand why the otters laughed even as they cheered.

Next he must learn to fish, they said.

"Fish? Well, I can try."

Pipsolk was already fretting about the fact that it was long past his usual dinner time.

"Patience," said the rabbit, trying to recall how otters fished. They dived first. Yes, that was the hard part. It meant ducking one's head right under the water. Never mind, if an otter could do it, so could a rabbit. And he ducked his head in the manner of otters and muskrats, hoisting his other end high up in the air so the little round tail would follow him down under the waves. Once upside down, with water in his nose and his ears and his eyes, the rabbit thought only of getting up to the surface again. He came up choking and spluttering, and oh didn't the air taste good!

"This way of fishing," he decided, "is not for me. Now, let me see, how do the bears go about it? I think they catch fish by just scooping them out of the water. I can do that, surely." So, standing in water up to his chin, Ableegumooch reached for a

leaping frog, made a swipe at a devil's-darning-needle, grabbed at a trout flashing by—and missed all three, to the vast merriment of the otter family. Still the rabbit kept trying. He saw a fat insect alight on the branch of an Indian Pear Tree and at the same time a salmon swam into view. Trying to grab both at the same time, Ableegumooch stepped off into deep water and sank. Down he went and at the very bottom his long hind foot caught in a pile of brush. There he was held fast. In a dreadful panic, he kicked and twisted, trying to get free. As he fought, a brown shape flashed past him underwater, turned and came back. It was Keoonik!

Seeing his guilt clearly for the first time, Ableegumooch was sure the otter had come to take his revenge. Well, thought the rabbit, I suppose I deserve to die, but I'm not going to if I can help it—certainly not to please Keoonik! So he braced himself for one last effort, and at the same moment his foot was miraculously freed. He shot up to the surface, more than half-drowned, where Keoonik grabbed him and pushed him in no gentle fashion to the shore.

"False friend! Traitor!" growled the otter. "I ought to have left you there to perish!"

"Why didn't you?" gasped the rabbit, still coughing up water.

"Because drowning's too good for you," Keoonik grinned. "I'm waiting to see what Pipsolk does when he finds out he and his family must go hungry to bed tonight! Ah well—you'll make a good substitute, Ableegumooch. We otters are very fond of rabbit stew."

"I'm sorry I spoiled things for you with Nesoowa."

"You didn't," laughed the other. "Nesoowa says she will run away with me rather than marry you." Keoonik glanced hurriedly over his shoulder. "Here comes Pipsolk now, and he looks hungry! You'd better start running!"

After one look at Pipsolk's face, Ableegumooch would have been glad to take Keoonik's advice, but he couldn't. He was still too weak and breathless to run anywhere—and in such a strait, as usual, he thought of the Great Chief and whispered a plea for help.

Suddenly Glooscap—who comes as the wind comes and no man knows how—stood between Ableegumooch and the wrathful otter.

"Boasting again, Ableegumooch," said the Great Chief, who probably loved the rabbit best of all his creatures, "and see where it's got you!"

"I'm sorry to bother you, Master," the rabbit apologized. "It was sink or swim—and I've already tried swimming!"

Glooscap shook his head in despair, trying not to smile. He turned to the otter, who was now looking innocent, as if rabbit stew had never entered his mind.

"Pipsolk, I want you to forget all about breeding and background and such nonsense and just tell Ableegumooch frankly what you think of him as a son-in-law."

Pipsolk turned to the rabbit.

"The fact is, Ableegumooch, you may be good enough in your way, but your breeding and ancestors won't fill my children's mouths. You'll never do as a husband for my daughter. She would soon starve. Indeed, after experiencing your kind of son-in-law, I can see more virtue in Kcoonik's sort. I believe, if Nesoowa is willing, I shall give him a trial after all."

"There!" cried Ableegumooch. "I told you I'd help you,

Keoonik." But the otter had rushed away to find Nesoowa and tell her the good news.

Glooscap gave his rabbit a severe look. "I hope you have learned something from all this, Ableegumooch."

"Oh, I have," cried the rabbit. "I know now I'm not cut out for swimming and fishing. From now on, I shall be satisfied just to be what I am, the handsomest, the cleverest, and best-bred rabbit in the world! And—" as an afterthought, "the best matchmaker!"

Whereupon to the rabbit's surprise Glooscap began to laugh, and he laughed so hard that all the trees bent with the gust of his laughter, and Ableegumooch had to cling to the Master's leg to keep from being blown away.

And there, *kespeadooksit,* our tale ends.

How the Human People Got the First Fire

by George Clutesi

Long, long time ago the human people had no fire.
There was no fire to cook the food,
The people ate their food cold.
There was no fire to dry their clothes,
No fire to warm them at winter time.
There was no fire to give them light when the moon would not.

It has been said there was no fire at all amongst the human people.
No one had fire, except the Wolf people.

The Wolf people were the most dreaded people in all the land.

"No other people shall ever have our fire," they would say, and
they guarded it with care, for they alone owned the precious fire.

"No one shall have it," they declared.

The human people wanted and needed the fire very much.
Great chiefs and their wise councillors would sit and make plans,
and more plans to find a way in which to capture the wondrous
fire.

"Let us call all the strong and brave men," the wise men would
say.

So the great chiefs from all the land would command that all
men come forward and try to capture the fire. The strongest would
boast that he would go forth to the land of the Wolf people and

force his way into their village and bring the fire back. He was strong. The brave knew no fear. He would go forth and capture the fire.

The wise one would say, "I will find a way to win the fire. I am wise."

The fastest would boast, "I will run off with the fire and bring it here to you all. I am fast."

One by one they would go out to capture the fire, and one by one they would come back with the same story. It cannot be done!

The strongest would say, "I could not even get near the village of the dreadful Wolves. They have guards all over the place of the fire. No one can ever enter their village. We can never have the fire. The Wolves are too smart for us."

The fastest would say, "I got so close to their village that I could smell the food roasting in their great fires, but I could not enter their great house."

The wise old one would say, "I'll think of a way."

The great chief was very sad. His best men had failed him and all the people of the land.

"What shall we do? What can we do? We shall be cold again this winter. We shall again eat cold, raw food. We shall be blind by night when the moon will not give us light, and there is no fire to light the way. We must have the fire! We must!" cried the great chief in despair.

No one spoke. No one moved. All eyes were cast down. All had tried and all had failed. All the people were very sad indeed.

But there was really no great need for sadness, for all the while the great council had met—the many trials to capture the fire—young Ah-tush-mit, Son of Deer, had the real secret of how to procure the fire from the Wolf people.

All throughout the great struggle for the possession of the fire Ah-tush-mit had been gambolling about the beach, racing, leaping and hopping about on his long spindly legs. He had seemingly paid no heed to all the great fuss about the fire.

He was racing past the people, as he had done so many times before, when suddenly he stopped directly in front of the chief and announced very simply in a small, small voice, "I'll get you the fire."

"You will what? What did that little boy say?" There was anger in the loud queries from the great braves and the strong men.

Then from the foolhardy ones a loud hee-haw went up—"Ho-ho-ho-ho-ho-ho."

"I'll get you the fire," the small boy repeated quite unabashed and not a bit frightened of the braves and the strong men, for he knew they had all tried and had failed to capture the fire.

Looking the great chief full in the face, Ah-tush-mit repeated again, "I'll get you the fire."

The little boy stood there, so small, so tiny and foolish looking among the great strong men. The wise chief was solemn while the others chuckled and laughed.

Ah-tush-mit, the Son of Deer, began twitching his long, long ears and rolling his big eyes as he looked this way and that way—but still he held his ground.

"I'll get you the fire," he persisted.

At last the great chief looked up and said, "Choo—all right—Ah-tush-mit, my strongest, bravest, fastest and wisest have all failed. Do the best you can."

Ah-tush-mit called the womenfolk together.

"Make me the most colourful costume you can," he commanded. "I am going to dance for the great Wolf chief."

"Dance? Who wants to dance at a time like this?" all the women wanted to know. "The boy is really foolish. He is wasting our time," they all declared.

"Obey and do everything Ah-tush-mit says," the wise old chief commanded his people. "Let the boy try. Give him a chance as I did to all of you," he continued.

Thus the womenfolk made him a head-band, a sash for his belt, bands for his knees and elbows, and for his ankles too. All these were made from the inner bark of the cedar tree, and dyed the colour of the young cohoe salmon—as red as red can be.

Ah-tush-mit fitted and worked with his regalia until it was just right. He paid especial attention to the bands for his knees. He kept remarking these knee-bands had to fit exactly right—not too tight, not too loose—just right so that he could dance well for the great Wolves.

While he was paying special attention to the knee-bands no one noticed that he tucked something into them between the bark and his skin. He worked with the knee-bands and finally they were smooth and exactly to his liking.

"Now I want the best drummers and singers," he announced. "Come with me to the outskirts of the Wolf village. Do not enter with me. When I give the signal you must all run back home as fast as you can.

"We shall go before dark so that you can reach your homes before the night blinds you," he assured the brave men and women drummers and singers who were to risk their very lives to accompany him to the outskirts of the Wolf village.

At last everything was in readiness. Evening came. Ah-tush-mit sallied forth to capture the fire for the human people from the most dreaded people in the land, the Wolf people.

"Show yourselves. Do not hide or sneak in any manner," he warned. "The Wolf people are wise and cunning. They would be sure to see us anyway, even if we were to try and sneak in by the dark of the night."

So the odd little company sang and beat their drums with all their might and main. The Wolf people heard them from a long distance off they sang so lustily. One strange thing took place. Ah-tush-mit did not take the lead as everyone had expected. Instead he hid himself behind the company of drummers.

"Ah, the foolish boy is now too frightened to show himself?" the women asked one another.

Finally the group of singers and drummers reached the outskirts

of the great village of the dreaded Wolves. The huge doors of the house opened slowly, and the biggest, fiercest-looking Wolves bounded out to see what all the noise and din was about.

The humans could see the large fire burning and blazing inside the great house of the Wolves. They could almost feel the heat and the smoke smelled so sweet as they inhaled with all their might, for they had never before seen or smelled the fire.

What a wondrous beautiful sight! Great sparks burst and escaped through the smoke hole on the top of the great roof. What a wonderful thing! So bright and beautiful in the gathering gloom of the dark night. These were the thoughts that ran through the minds of the awe-stricken humans.

Suddenly Ah-tush-mit sprang forward from his place of concealment. He was on all fours as he began his dance. He sidled towards the door of the great Wolf house. It was fast getting dark. The flickering light from the fire reached out to him and cast pleasing shadows all around as he danced and sprang about on his four spindly legs. Suddenly, he made the signal and the singers and drummers stopped their din abruptly and fled for home as they had been instructed.

Little Ah-tush-mit was left all alone with the fire and the fierce Wolves. There were no more drums nor singers to give him courage, and he was very frightened. He was very, very frightened indeed.

He could hear the Wolf chief asking, "What is all the noise about?"

A Wolf guard answered, "It is only young Ah-tush-mit dancing."

"Send him away," the chief growled.

"Ah, what a jolly little boy! Bring him in. Do let him in," the Wolf chief's wife called out.

"Let us see him dance for awhile, then send him home," the chief agreed.

Ah-tush-mit increased the pace of his dance. Towards the great

40

doors he pranced, hopping straight up and down, with no bend to his knees. Hop, hop, hop, hop, he went, sidling ever closer to the opening of the doorway, and as he circled around he sang a rollicking ditty:

Kiyaaa tlin, tlin, tlin, tlin,
Kiyaaa tlin, tlin, tlin, tlin,
Ooo nootl sahshh keeyah-qwa-yup qwatlin,
Hee yah ahh haaa ya-yaulk tah khaus ti-nah-is,
Kiyaaa tlin, tlin, tlin, tlin,
Kiyaaa, tlin, tlin, tlin, tlin.

Break, crack, crack, crack, crack,
Break, crack, crack, crack, crack,
Do I break yon stakes with these I wear?
My flints, my sandstone hooves,
Break, crack, crack, crack, crack,
Break, crack, crack, crack, crack.

Ah-tush-mit's voice was small, but he sang with all his heart. He sang with all his might. He was singing to capture a spark. Ah-tush-mit was singing for his life!

Hop, hop, hop, hop, stiff-legged, he entered the doors. Once inside he could see the fire burning brightly and all about it was a bed of stakes made of broken bones implanted into the earth, as sharp as mussel shells they were. This was what his little song was all about. Up to this very minute no human who had ever tried to get past that awful bed of bone stakes had lived to tell the tale.

Ah-tush-mit danced with all his heart. He danced as he had never danced before. He danced so he might capture a tiny spark. Ah-tush-mit danced for his life.

"Kiyaaa tlin, tlin, tlin, tlin," he sang as he sidled ever closer towards the awful trap made with broken bones. Skirting its edges in a half circle, he danced towards a far corner, closer to the fire,

41

but where the bones were neither so large nor too plentiful in the ground.

Suddenly he had arrived at his chosen spot and with a mighty leap he was among the broken bones, hopping higher and ever higher as he picked his way among the sharp spear-like bones. His sharp little feet seemed to fit around and pass between the dangerous bones harmlessly. His long shanks and slim legs kept his plump little body safely away from the sharp, sharp points and thus he was saved from being torn to shreds.

"Do I break yon stakes of bones with these I wear? My flints, my sandstone hooves?" he sang.

The Wolf people were completely fascinated. Their big and awful jaws hung open in wonderment. Ah-tush-mit had won the cheers and applause of the Wolf people.

The little fellow's bright costume glowed in the firelight.

"Break, crack, crack, crack, crack," his little song floated over the great fire. "With these I wear my flints, my sandstone hooves," he carolled as he suddenly sprang right beside the great fire.

Ah-tush-mit sang louder and louder, he leaped higher and ever higher; he was dancing to capture a spark; he was dancing for his very life.

"Ah, what a jolly little boy! He is a dancer, a good dancer," the mamma Wolf beamed.

Then it happened—as quick as a flash—before your eyes could blink. Ah-tush-mit had turned towards the roaring fire and with a mighty leap he sailed into the air—right over the roaring fire sailed he.

"Ho-ho-ho-ho-ho," roared the Wolves. "Ah-tush-mit is on fire. Ho-ho-ho-ho-ho."

Ah-tush-mit had indeed caught on fire. His little legs smouldered between the knees. He stopped his dancing and bounded through the great doors with a mighty leap. Once clear of the great Wolf house he raced for his life towards home as fast as he could run.

All around the leaping, roaring fire the Wolves sat bemused. The whole action of little Ah-tush-mit had happened so quickly and seemingly without intent that they were taken completely by surprise. Before they realized what had occurred Ah-tush-mit was well away from the Wolf village. Ah-tush-mit, the Son of Deer, the fleetest of them all, had completely outsmarted the Wolves, the most dreaded people of the land.

With a spark smouldering between his knees he had captured the fire! With his sharp pointed feet, his flints and sandstone hooves he had successfully run the sharp broken stakes of bones.

Yes indeed, with his colourful costume, his captivating dance, he had outwitted the most cunning people of the land. Ah-tush-mit, Son of Deer, the small one, had captured the fire for the human people.

The secret something Ah-tush-mit had tucked between his knees had been a small bundle of very dry sticks he had gathered from the undermost branches of the spruce tree. It was this that had caught fire since it was dry as dry can be, and even some of the spruce gum still stuck to the twigs. When the sticks caught fire the cedar bark bands had smouldered until he reached home with the tiny sparks of fire. This was where the tinder had come from and where the human people first came to know about fire.

But Ah-tush-mit had burned himself. The inside of his knees were badly scorched. Thus it is to this day that the inside of all deers' knees are singed black. That is how the human people got their first fire.

In the growing season, when all living things burst out in bloom
Sit in the glade of the wood at even-tide.
If your own heart be open to love be there for Ah-tush-mit
You will hear the thump and the beat of his little song:
Thump, thump, thump, thump.

The Girl Who Married the Morning Star

by Frances Fraser

On a hot summer night, in a long-ago time, three young girls were lying on the grass by the river, talking, as young girls do, of the men they would marry some day. One, daughter of a chief, the most beautiful of the three, found fault with every man suggested by the others. At last, exasperated, they said to her, "What do you want for a husband—a star? No man pleases you!"

The girl raised her eyes to the sky, where one star shone brighter than all the rest. "I would marry that star if he would come and get me. I wish he would! Please come, Star!" The girls laughed, and returned to their tepees.

When night came again, there was need of wood, to feed the campfires, and the girls were sent to gather some.

While they were picking up the dried branches, a young man dressed in beautiful feathered garments stepped out of a thicket, and said to the daughter of the chief, "Are you ready to go?"

"Go? Go where?" she said. "Who are you?"

"I am the Star you called last night," the stranger said. "You offered to marry me, remember? I have come to take you to my home in the Sky Country."

The girl looked at him. He was tall, and strong, and his eyes were kind. She turned to her companions, and said to them, "Tell my parents where I have gone." And the other girls, frightened, ran toward the camp.

The Star Man took a robe, made of feathers, and coloured like the rainbow, from his back, and, wrapping it round the girl, held her close against him. And they rose through the air toward the Sky Country.

It was a beautiful country. There were green grass, and flowers and berries, and quiet-running water. There was neither sickness, nor pain; the lodges never wore out, nor the clothing; there was always food, just by wishing for it—and the winter never came. The women had only to do what work they wished, and the men spent all their time on raids, and war. But those who were killed always, by daylight next morning, were alive again. And the animals were tame, and easy to hunt. It was a beautiful country.

The girl forgot all about her people and her life on the earth. After a while a son was born to them, and her happiness was complete.

Only one thing was forbidden. Her husband had told her that never was she to pull up a certain large wild turnip (ma'ase') that grew in a hollow near their tepee. For a long time she respected the restriction, but more and more she wondered, Why? What would happen if she did? The thought grew and grew.

One day her husband went hunting; and as she sat in the tepee with nothing to do, she thought of the ma'ase'. And she went to the hollow and pulled it up.

The ma'ase' left a hole in the sky, and looking down through it, she saw a circle of lodges, with the people going about the daily tasks of the camp. A wave of homesickness poured over her—a nostalgia for the life she had left, for the gossip of the women, the familiar tasks, the noise and smells of the camp. She replaced the ma'ase', and went, weeping, to her lodge.

Her husband, returning, found her sobbing in the tepee. "You

disobeyed me," he said, sadly. "Now, I must send you back to your people." He sent messengers to gather hides of buffalo, hundreds of them, all the Star people had. Then they cut each hide into long strips, and tied them together, making a long, long rope.

They lowered the girl and her baby down to the earth. But the baby was changed into a large mushroom, or puff-ball (which our people call "Star-Balls") since, being a sky-child, he could not live on the earth.

With her the girl also brought the Sacred Turnip, the ma'ase', and on her head she wore the holy Crown, the head-dress used to this day by the woman who makes the Sun Dance. (And to this day, the ma'ase' has a part in those rituals, and the poles of the Sun Lodge are tied with rawhide rope.)

The girl lived with her family, teaching the people much that she had learned in the Sky Country. She tended her Star baby.

But among the people were some who resented her teaching. And one day, these wicked ones took the Star baby, and cut it up into small pieces, and scattered the bits around on the ground.

The girl was heartbroken at the killing of her Star baby. When the Morning Star rose next, she went out on the prairie and called to her husband, asking him if the ones who did this could not be punished.

He answered her, and told her to have her father and other men build a raft of logs tied with thongs. When the raft was completed, they were to take a pair of each kind of animal on to the raft, and to warn the virtuous members of her tribe to go there too.

Then the Star sent moon after moon of rain, till all the earth was flooded. The people and animals on the raft were all that were left alive.

When the rain had ceased, the girl's father sent a young beaver to find land. The beaver never came back.

Later, the chief sent a duck out. The duck, too, did not return. He sent other birds, and other water animals, and they, also were not seen again.

At last, the muskrat said, "Let me go." The chief protested. He was fond of the muskrat, and the others had not come back. But the girl added her voice to that of the muskrat and at last the chief consented, and the little animal departed.

Late in the night, a feeble splashing was heard alongside the raft. The muskrat, nearly dead from exhaustion, had come back, and clutched in one little paw was a tiny bit of earth.

The water was receding, and at last the green grass grew again, and the flood was over. (The water went into the rivers, and the lakes, and down into holes and crevices in the ground. That's why, when you dig a well, you get water.)

The girl saw her people happy again, leading lives of virtue, with due attention given to the things she had taught them. But she was lonely, and when the Morning Star shone bright, she went out and called him, and the Star Man came for her as he had before, and they went back to their home in the Sky Country.

Heaven and Hell
an Eskimo poem

And when we die at last,
we really know very little about what happens then.
But people who dream
have often seen the dead appear to them
just as they were in life.
Therefore we believe life does not end here on earth.

We have heard of three places where men go after death:
There is the Land of the Sky, a good place
where there is no sorrow and fear.
There have been wise men who went there
and came back to tell us about it:
They saw people playing ball, happy people
who did nothing but laugh and amuse themselves.
What we see from down here in the form of stars
are the lighted windows of the villages of the dead
in the Land of the Sky.

Then there are two other worlds of the dead underground:
Way down deep is a place just like here on earth
except on earth you starve
and down there they live in plenty.
The caribou graze in great herds
and there are endless plains
with juicy berries that are nice to eat.
Down there too, everything
is happiness and fun for the dead.

But there is another place, the Land of the Miserable,
right under the surface of the earth we walk on.
There go all the lazy men who were poor hunters,
and all women who refused to be tattooed,
not caring to suffer a little to become beautiful.
They had no life in them when they lived
so now after death they must squat on their haunches
with hanging heads, bad-tempered and silent,
and live in hunger and idleness
because they wasted their lives.
Only when a butterfly comes flying by
do they lift their heads
(as young birds open pink mouths uselessly after a gnat)
and when they snap at it, a puff of dust
comes out of their dry throats.

Of course it may be
that all I have been telling you is wrong
for you cannot be certain about what you cannot see.
But these are the stories that our people tell.

The Boy in the Land of Shadows

by Cyrus Macmillan

Two orphan children, a boy and a girl, lived alone near the mountains. Their parents had long been dead and the children were left to look after themselves without any kindred upon the earth. The boy hunted all day long and provided much food, and the girl kept the house in order and did the cooking. They had a very deep love for each other and as they grew up they said, "We shall never leave each other. We shall always stay here together." But one year it happened that in the early spring-time it was very cold. The snow lingered on the plains and the ice moved slowly from the rivers and chill winds were always blowing and grey vapours hovered over all the land. And there was very little food to be had, for the animals hid in their warm winter dens and the wild-geese and ducks were still far south. And in this cruel period of bad weather the little girl sickened and died. Her brother worked hard to provide her with nourishing food and he gathered all the medicine roots he thought could bring her relief, but it was all to no purpose. And despite all his efforts, one evening in the twilight his sister went away to the West, leaving him alone behind upon the earth.

The boy was heart-broken because of his sister's death. And when the late spring came and the days grew warm and food was plentiful again, he said, "She must be somewhere in the West, for they say that our people do not really die. I will go and search for her, and perhaps I can find her and bring her back." So one morning he set out on his strange quest. He journeyed many days westward towards the Great Water, killing game for food as he went, and sleeping at night under the stars. He met many strange people, but he did not tell them the purpose of his travels. At last he came to the shore of the Great Water, and he sat looking towards the sunset wondering what next to do. In the evening an old man came along. "What are you doing here?" asked the man. "I am looking for my sister," said the boy; "some time ago she sickened and died and I am lonely without her, and I want to find her and bring her back." And the man said, "Some time ago she whom you seek passed this way. If you wish to find her you must undertake a dangerous journey." The boy answered that he would gladly risk any dangers to find his sister, and the old man said, "I will help you. Your sister has gone to the Land of Shadows far away in the Country of Silence which lies out yonder in the Island of the Blest. To reach the Island you must sail far into the West, but I warn you that it is a perilous journey, for the crossing is always rough and your boat will be tossed by tempests. But you will be well repaid for your trouble, for in that land nobody is ever hungry or tired; there is no death and no sorrow; there are no tears, and no one ever grows old."

Then the old man gave the boy a large pipe and some tobacco and said, "This will help you in your need." And he brought him to where a small canoe lay dry upon the beach. It was a wonderful canoe, the most beautiful the boy had ever seen. It was cut from a single white stone and it sparkled in the red twilight like a polished jewel. And the old man said, "This canoe will weather all storms. But see that you handle it carefully, and when you come back see that you leave it in the cove where you found it."

Soon afterwards, the boy set out on his journey. The moon was full and the night was cold with stars. He sailed into the West over a rough and angry sea, but he was in no danger, for his canoe rode easily on the waters. All around him he saw in the moonlight many other canoes going in the same direction and all white and shining like his own. But no one seemed to be guiding them, and although he looked long at them not a person could he make out. He wondered if the canoes were drifting unoccupied, for when he called to them there was no answer. Sometimes a canoe upset in the tossing sea and the waves rose over it and it was seen no more, and the boy often thought he heard an anguished cry. For several days he sailed on to the West, and all the time other canoes were not far away, and all the time some of them were dropping from sight beneath the surging waters, but he saw no people in them.

At last, after a long journey, the sea grew calm and the air was sweet and warm. There was no trace of the storm, for the waves were quiet and the sky was as clear as crystal. He saw that he was near the Island of the Blest of which the old man had spoken, for it was now plain to his view, as it rose above the ocean, topped with green grass and trees, and a snow-white beach. Soon he reached the shore and drew up his canoe. As he turned away he came upon a skeleton lying flat upon the sand. He stopped to look at it, and as he did so, the skeleton sat up and said in great surprise, "You should not be here. Why have you come?" And the boy said, "I seek my sister. In the early spring-time she sickened and died, and I am going to the Land of Shadows in the Country of Silence in search of her." "You must go far inland," said the skeleton, "and the way is hard to find for such as you." The boy asked for guidance and the skeleton said, "Let me smoke and I will help you." The boy gave him the pipe and tobacco he had received from the old man, and he laughed when he saw his strange companion with the pipe between his teeth. The skeleton smoked for some time and at last, as the smoke rose from his pipe, it changed to a flock of little white birds, which flew about like doves. The boy

looked on in wonder, and the skeleton said, "These birds will guide you. Follow them." Then he gave back the pipe and stretched out again flat upon the sand, and the boy could not arouse him from his sleep.

The boy followed the little white birds as he had been told. He went along through a land of great beauty where flowers were blooming and countless birds were singing. Not a person did he meet on the way. The place was deserted except for the song-birds and the flowers. He passed through the Country of Silence, and came to a mysterious land where no one dwelt. But although he saw no one he heard many voices and he could not tell whence they came. They seemed to be all around him. At last the birds stopped at the entrance to a great garden, and flew around his head in a circle. They would go no further and they alighted on a tree close by, all except one, which perched on the boy's shoulder. The lad knew that here at last was the Land of Shadows.

When he entered the garden he heard again many low voices. But he saw no one. He saw only many shadows of people on the grass, but he could not see from what the shadows came. He wondered greatly at the strange and unusual sight, for back in his homeland in that time the sunlight made no shadows. He listened again to the voices and he knew now that the shadows were speaking. He wandered about for some time marvelling greatly at the strange place with its weird unearthly beauty. At last he heard a voice which he knew to be his sister's. It was soft and sweet, just as he had known it when they were together on the earth, and it had not changed since she left him. He went to the shadow from which the voice came, and throwing himself on the grass beside it, he said, "I have long sought you, my sister. I have come to take you home. Let me see you as you were when we dwelt together." But his sister said, "You have done wisely to keep me in your memory, and to seek to find me. But here we cannot appear to the people of earth except as shadows. I cannot go back with you, for it is now too late. I have eaten of the food of this land; if you had

come before I had eaten, perhaps you could have taken me away. Who knows? But my heart and my voice are unchanged, and I still remember my dear ones, and with unaltered love I still watch my old home. And although I cannot go to you, you can some day come to me. First you must finish your work on earth. Go back to your home in the Earth Country. You will become a great Chief among your people. Rule wisely and justly and well, and give freely of your food to the poor among the Indians who have not as much as you have. And when your work on earth is done you shall come to me in this Land of Shadows beyond the Country of Silence, and we shall be together again and our youth and strength and beauty will never leave us."

And the boy, wondering greatly and in deep sorrow, said, "Let me stay with you now." But his sister said, "That cannot be." Then she said, "I will give you a Shadow, which you must keep with you as your guardian spirit. And while you have it with you, no harm can come to you, for it will be present only in the Light, and where there is Light there can be no wickedness. But when it disappears you must be on your guard against doing evil, for then there will be darkness, and darkness may lead you to wrong."

So the boy took the Shadow, and said good-bye for a season and set out on his homeward journey. The little white birds, which had waited for him in the trees, guided him back to the beach. His canoe was still there, but the skeleton-man had gone and there was not a trace of him to be found upon the sand. And the Island of the Blest was silent except for the songs of the birds and the ripple of the little streams. The boy embarked in his canoe and sailed towards the east, and as he pushed off from the beach the little white birds left him and disappeared in the air. The sea was now calm and there was no storm, as there had been on his outward journey. Soon he reached the shore on the other side. He left his canoe in the cove as the old man had told him, and in a few days he arrived at his home, still bearing the Shadow from the Country of Silence.

He worked hard for many years but he did no evil, and in the end he became a great Chief and did much good for his people. He ruled wisely and justly and well, as his sister had commanded him. Then one day, when he was old and his work was done, he disappeared, and his people knew that he had gone to join his sister in the Land of Shadows in the Country of Silence far away somewhere in the West. But he left behind him the Shadow his sister had given him; and while there is Light the Indians still have their Shadow and no harm can come to them, for where there is Light there can be no evil.

But always in the late autumn the Shadows of the Indian brother and sister in the Country of Silence are lonely for their former life. And they think of their living friends and of the places of their youth, and they wish once more to follow the hunt, for they know that the hunter's moon is shining. And when their memory dwells with longing on their earlier days, their spirits are allowed to come back to earth for a brief season from the Land of Shadows. Then the winds are silent and the days are very still, and the smoke of their camp fires appears like haze upon the air. And men call this season Indian Summer, but it is really but a Shadow of the golden summer that has gone. And it always is a reminder to the Indians that in the Land of Shadows, far away in the Country of Silence in the West, there are no dead.

Voices
in the Wilderness

A Shipwreck

by W. Percival Way

On Christmas Day, 1850, the "Niobe," with a crew of eight persons, under the command of Captain Robinson, set sail from Leghorn, with a gentle breeze, bound for Cadiz. Arriving there, we took in our cargo, which consisted chiefly of salt, and on January 14th received orders to go to Newfoundland. Accordingly, the next morning we set sail, with a fair wind and every prospect of making a quick trip.

We sighted land on the evening of February 29th, after having encountered a very severe storm in crossing the Atlantic. The next morning I ascended the maintop, and the first thing that met my view was a light. I instantly called the captain, who said that it was the light of Cape Spear (Newfoundland).

About sunset, as we passed Bacalieu, things began to assume a different aspect. The wind, instantly changing, began to blow violently. In the meantime the snow was falling so thickly that we could scarcely see the jib-boom.

We then received orders to close-reef, clear the decks—as everything gave evidence that a storm was fast approaching. In a short time the wind had risen to a perfect gale.

The vessel being now close-reefed every man was on the watch, looking out for land. We were scudding at a rapid rate when I happened to glance toward the head of the vessel, where everything appeared to look dark. I called out to the captain and asked him if that was land ahead. At the same moment "Starboard the helm and bring her to" rang from the lips of the half-frantic captain. "I see land all around us. We are lost! We are lost!" he again shouted. Each one in a moment realized his fate. I was at the helm. I held it till she struck, which carried away all the foremost part. I then let it go, and threw off both my coats. The vessel by this time had receded a little with the sea, but only to be precipitated with greater force against the cliff, carrying away the taffrail with the shock.

Now a very pathetic scene presented itself. Men who, but a few hours before, were even cursing God and their existence, could now be seen crying to God for Mercy. I managed to cut the ropes which bound the jolly-boat to the ship's side. The mate and three others went below to die. The captain, Billy, George and myself stood out for life. About the hardest thing that ever I endured was to hear poor little Billy screaming, and asking me to save him.

George and I then went aft to get a block ready to hoist the jolly-boat on the outer side. Just as we had it ready, and were almost down, the vessel came in with such a crash as broke the foremast off, and both of us fell to the deck, having narrowly escaped being killed. At this moment a tremendous sea broke over us, causing them that were under to rush on deck. Just as we had the boat ready and all were on board except myself, who was holding the painter, another sea came, which swept the jolly-boat across the ship, turning her bottom up, and throwing all of us into the water.

As I was being tossed about on the waves I felt my back touch something. I seized it, turned over, and got my head above water. In a moment, although almost unconscious, I realized my situation. I climbed to the top of the mast, and when the vessel touched the cliff again I jumped and caught hold of a shiver with my fingers. In that manner I remained hanging, till I found a place to rest my feet.

Imagine my position, gentle reader, if you can: In the middle of the night, dripping with wet and half-benumbed with the cold, holding on to a shiver of a perpendicular cliff several hundred feet in height with my fingers, and a narrow ledge about four inches wide to rest my feet on. Below me were the warring waves, dashing with united fury against the cliff, and at times would run so high as almost to wash me away.

While I was holding on in this manner I heard the vessel coming in again, and by inclining my body a little to the left I saved my life, which would have been lost by a stroke from the masthead. A tremendous sea then came and broke with such fury over me that I almost fell a victim to it. As I was trying to wipe the water from my eyes I heard the vessel coming in again; and while I was thinking whether I would be killed this time or not I heard somebody coming up the rigging. In a few moments I found it was my friend

George. As soon as the vessel touched again he jumped, and, as happened, a little way beyond me. I soon made myself known to him. He then told me that all the crew were lost. I told him that I would soon be gone too, as I could not hold out much longer. He then told me that I must try and get up where he was, as he did not need to hold on at all, but had a large shelf to rest on.

All that we then heard was the howling of the winds, the roaring of the waves, and the vessel beating against the cliff. It seemed to me the longest night I ever spent on earth. In the morning I could scarcely hold on. My friend then told me that he had a ball of spun-yarn in his pocket. He got it ready, threw it to me, holding one end in his hand. Then, thinking that I would be too heavy, I managed to slip off my boots and pants, and, by God's help and my own, I got up all right.

We felt thankful to be together again, although the worst had not then come. The night was piercing cold, and I had hardly any clothing on. The next two days and nights we managed to keep in good spirits, but, as we saw no way of deliverance, things began to look gloomy, and my comrade, getting so discouraged, laid himself down to die. It was a hard time with me. I held him on my arm for the next three days and nights, blowing my breath to his heart. He talked much of his friends having plenty, and he without anything. Once in the night I heard him exclaim, "Cook, give me something to eat, or I'll tell the captain on you." I shook him, and when I got him a little sensible I tried to impress the idea on him that the captain and cook were lost, that we were on the cliff, and that I had no food to give him. He was deathly pale, and told me that he was going to die. "George," said I, "if you die I'll eat you." "O John," he exclaimed, "for God's sake don't eat me." With that thought stamped on his mind he kept alive till daybreak, and, thank God, it was the last daybreak we saw in that miserable abode. All that night I was trying to think of some way of escape. When the sun had risen I lifted him from my arm, and told him that I was going to leave him. "O John," said he, "don't leave;

don't leave me." I took a last look, as I thought, at him, and then left him.

When I had got a little way beyond him my hands began to fail me. I looked at them and found that they were frozen. I felt as if I could hold on no longer. So I got my chin to rest on a shiver, and in that manner bore the weight of my body for some minutes. On my right, a few feet from me, I saw a place that, if I got there, I could rest as long as I chose. I asked God to help me, and, after a great difficulty, I succeeded. Then I sat down and began to think. I knew I would not be able to climb any more, for my hands were severely frost-bitten. I put them in my armpits and began to squeeze them, moaning bitterly.

While I was busy watching my eye was directed to a dark object, which appeared to move. In a very short time I found that it was a boat. It had been on the search for seals, and through a suggestion from one of the crew, determined to row around the shore on the way home.

Fearing that we should be passed unobserved I began shouting at the top of my voice. Being attracted by the sound the little boy on board began to look in all directions. It was not long before he saw me, and told his father that up in the cliff he could see an owl and hear it screeching.

To satisfy the boy's curiosity, the boat's head was turned directly towards the spot. In a short time all their doubts had disappeared, for they could see, and hear me shouting. After explaining the matter to them, they left us to get assistance. They soon returned, however, and in a comparatively short time we were taken down and carried to comfortable quarters, where, under careful nursing, we remained for some time.

Space would not permit me to enter into the details of the story. Suffice to say, that, after three weeks, with my hands partly well, I left for home, leaving my friend with both legs amputated. From our parting then we have never seen nor heard from each other since.

The Fisher Who Died in His Bed
a song from Newfoundland

Old Jim Jones the fisher, the trapper, the trawler,
Jim Jones the fish-killin' banker is dead.
No fisherman surely never stepped in a dory
Like Jim Jones the fisher who died in his bed.

Was there any old fellow tied sods or made bobbers
And set out his trawls in the dark it is said?
No fisherman ever braved such stormy weather
Like Jim Jones the trawler who died in his bed.

Jim Jones he would shorely go out in a dory
And set out his traps all weighed down with lead.
No fisher from side on hauled traps with such tide on
As Jim Jones the trapper who died in his bed.

In the foggiest of weather he'd set out the leader,
But who in the devil this side of the Head
Could haul up such codfish or pick out the dogfish
Like old Skipper Jones who died in his bed?

There was never such a salter this side of the water,
And ne'er such a glutton for eatin' cods' heads
There ne'er was a crackie who could chaw tobaccy
Like old Skipper Jones who died in his bed.

Was there any old fisher or any old fellow
Cut throats or split fish or tear off the head?
I'm darned if I ever saw one who'd pick liver
So fast as our skipper who died in his bed.

66

Is there any old fellow this side of the harbour
Sailed straight out the harbour or tacked round the Head
It would make you all frantic to sail the Atlantic
With old Skipper Jones who died in his bed.

His fishing days ended, his traps are unmended,
His trawls are all rotten, his fishing boat sunk.
His days as a rover are finished and over—
Old Skipper Jim Jones who died in his bunk.

How the Main John Got His Name

by Lorrie McLaughlin

The Main John is a loggin' man from the moment he breathes his first breath and he'll be a loggin' man until he breathes his last. They say that when the Main John was born his pa takes one look at the lad and says, "Cut me down the tallest tree in New Brunswick and give it to the lad for a teething ring."

So the men go out, one after the other, lookin' for a tree tall enough and fine enough for the Main John to be cuttin' his teeth on and finally they bring back the tallest tree in the world and drop it down beside him.

The Main John looks at it and he puts his hands around it and his pa shouts out, "That's a teethin' ring meant for a loggin' man, if ever I saw one!"

And before anyone so much as blinks an eye, the Main John chews that log into toothpicks and spits them out in as neat a pile as ever any man had seen.

"He's a loggin' man, sure enough," says the Main John's pa and he tosses his two-bladed axe into the trunk of a tree. "No man's to be touching that axe except the boy here, when he's ready."

The axe stays there in the tree, waitin', and every once in a while some smart lumberjack comes along, thinkin' the axe is meant for him, but try as they do, none of them ever so much as budges it in the back.

"See," says the men who were there the day the Main John was born, "it's meant for the lad and nobody else!"

When the Main John is four or so, he decides it's time he set to work like everybody else and he starts through the woods, lookin' for the spot where his pa sank that axe. He finds it right off, too, because he's got a way in the woods and he's not one to get himself lost, the Main John isn't.

He stands there, lookin' at his pa's axe, and one of the lumberjacks who tried to pull out the axe and couldn't starts in laughin'.

"Back to the nursery, lad," he shouts. "Loggin' is work for men!"

The Main John looks as if he didn't even hear. He spits on his hands and he grabs hold of that axe handle and he gives it a pull that heaves up the tree and the earth around it so as there's a mountain where there never was one before, and he stands there with his pa's axe in his hand, shoutin', "Loggin' is work for *me!*" and there's not a man in the woods ready to argue the point with him.

After that, the Main John goes through the woods of New Brunswick like a buzz saw and by the time he's five or thereabouts, he's usin' a man's peavey hook and an axe as big as he is and there's not a tree in the forest he can't be cuttin' down with one swing.

There's not a man or a tree can stand in the way of the Main John and when he makes up his mind he wants a thing, it's as good as his.

"I think I'd like me some pancakes," he says one mornin' to the cook.

The cook thinks about it a bit and says, "That's all well and good but I don't have me a fry pan big enough to make pancakes to suit you!"

The Main John thinks about that for a second or so and then he shouts out for a fry pan bigger than any in the world. "No matter what it costs!" he shouts. "Get me a fry pan big enough to cook all the pancakes I can manage."

The cook starts runnin' as soon as the Main John starts to shout and he doesn't stop runnin' until he gets to Fredericton.

"I need me a fry pan!" he shouts. "Big enough to cook all the pancakes in the world!"

Nobody in town has ever seen a fry pan *that* big and the cook gets pretty upset because he knows he doesn't dare go back to the Main John without that fry pan. He runs all around Fredericton, shoutin' and lookin', and finally he spots a battleship anchored in the harbour.

The cook takes a look at that battleship and all its metal hull and its smokestacks risin' into the sky.

"That's what it takes to make a fry pan big enough to fry up all the pancakes in the world!" says the cook and before anybody knows what he's up to he starts shoutin' for all the loggin' men in town to give him a hand.

They work all day and all night, tearin' that battleship apart with their bare hands, and by dawn they've got the biggest fry pan anybody has ever seen, and they start in carryin' it back to the Main John.

Then everybody stands around while the cook starts mixin' up the batter and pourin' those pancakes out of a boiler and nobody watches closer than the Main John himself.

He starts eatin' those pancakes as soon as they're cooked, and by the next mornin' he's startin' to slow down a bit, and by sundown he says, "Now, that's what I call a man-sized servin' of pancakes! You can fry me up a second helpin'!"

Somebody new to those parts looks at the Main John, not quite believin' what he sees, and he says, "No man livin' can eat that many pancakes!"

The cook hardly looks up from mixin' up the second servin' of pancakes but somebody else shouts, "John Glazier can!"

"John who?" demands the fellow new to those parts and before anybody else can say a word the Main John turns and looks at him.

"*I'm* who!" he says. "John Glazier. The Main John!"

The loggers standin' around watchin' and listen' nod their heads. "That's just who he is," they say. "The Main John!" and from then on nobody ever calls him anything else.

"The Berry Patch"

from *Westward Ho! 1903*
by Barbara Cormack

The Nesbitt family is crossing the country by wagon train to take up a new home out West. Many adventures happen to them along the way, and more than once they wish they were safe and secure back in England. Their little Indian friend, Johnny Yellowleaves, has gone berry-picking with them today.

As the summer went by, the newcomers found that their diet could be varied, for the better, by the use of the many wild berries that grew on the prairies. Mrs. Nesbitt remembered the canned saskatoons they had had at the home of Jim Morsby's cousins, and the stories they had told about the wealth of fruit. Johnny Yellowleaves was a great help in finding the berry patches, for he knew the type of land where they grew.

First, there were the strawberries, the tiny scarlet fruit on the low-lying plants hidden in the grass in open country. Mrs. Nesbitt was delighted.

"I've never known strawberries with such a flavour," she said. "And just think. We'll be able to have strawberries and cream every day for tea. What will the people at home have to say about that?"

Fred grumbled at the smallness of them. "They taste all right, but a chap spends half the morning getting a teacup full. Too hard on my old back."

The youngsters didn't mind. They lay down full length in the sweet-smelling grass, from which point of vantage they could see the scarlet drops of goodness in all directions.

After the strawberries came the raspberries. Johnny searched a long time before he found a good raspberry patch. "Grow where there's bush," he said. "Where fire's been through." He and Ted combed the surrounding countryside for days until they located such a spot. When they finally discovered the berries, they ate till they could eat no more, and took back samples in the tin pails they carried.

Next day they organized an expedition to the patch, with the Greens and Morgans going along, too. The wagon was loaded with pails, wash-tubs, and pans.

"We've been too greedy just eating up all this fruit," Mrs. Nesbitt told them firmly. "I'm going to make jam. Here, I got a letter from my sister last week, saying as how she's got a bargain on raspberries for the jam-making. I reckon our price will be a deal better than hers!"

The patch was situated in a clump of trees, near the grove from which they had got logs for the house, and it was a delightful spot for a picnic. A fire had evidently been through some years before, clearing away much of the underbrush, and the raspberry canes, well loaded with berries, were in full view.

Even Fred did not object to the raspberry picking. "At least a fellow can sit down on the job," he said. "You don't have to lie on your stomach to spot the things. And you can get the bottom of your pail covered before you get discouraged."

The others advanced upon the patch with shouts of pleasure. Each had his own special method of picking. Johnny was the explorer. He spent most of his time discovering good bushes, and directing the others to them. Ted and Lil at first ate far more than they put in the pails, but after a while they began to get sick of them, and then they settled down to the job more steadily.

There was a keen sense of competition.

"You half full yet?"

"Quarter full, about."

"I'm just an inch from the top!"

"Aw go on! Look at the size of the pail you've got. It's only about half as big as mine."

Mrs. Nesbitt discovered that the best method of picking was to get down on her knees and look up. "You see more that way, and don't miss them. I wager we'll be seeing rasps in our sleep tonight."

It was Lil who had the adventure. She had proved herself an excellent little picker, and stayed on the job like a veteran. Anxious to get her pail full before Ted filled his, she had discovered a very good patch farther up the trail. There were red berries everywhere she looked.

Periodically, Mrs. Nesbitt called out to check on her whereabouts.

"Lil! Lil! Where are you?"

Lil heard, but she did not reply. If she did, she knew Ted would be sent to fetch her, and she wanted to have a full pail when she met him.

"Lil, love. Answer me. Where are you?"

The sound of the voice, and the crackling of the underbrush told Lil that her mother was searching for her in the opposite direction. She kept silent. She'd get her pail full, and then run back and surprise them. She went on picking as fast as she could. The calls stopped.

The pail was full when she started back along the trail. She brushed her hand across her eyes. Things looked different. Or was it just because she had been looking at red raspberries too long?

Yes, that was the tree she had passed when she made her wonderful discovery. Or was it? Maybe the taller one farther down

was it. They looked very much alike. Not particularly worried, she went off in the direction of the spot where they had had their picnic, or so she thought.

"Mum! Dad! Ted!"

There was no answer.

She kept on walking in the same direction, not quite so confident. As the trail began to look less familiar, she grew worried, and her walk quickened into a run.

"Mum! Dad!"

Then, round the corner of a bush, she caught sight of her mother's dark skirt. Sobbing and breathless, she hurried round.

"Mum. Why didn't you shout?"

She let out a shriek. It wasn't Mum's dark skirt at all. There, standing on his hind legs picking raspberries with the best of them, was a big black bear! At the sound of the scream he got down clumsily and lumbered off down the trail, just as Johnny Yellowleaves and the others came racing down. Johnny had seen the bear and given warning. He was clashing two tins together.

"That'll frighten him," he explained. "Bears frighten easy most times."

Mrs. Nesbitt, thoroughly terrified, rushed to Lil and hugged her, then boxed her ears soundly for not answering when she was called.

"Thank God!" she said, in tears. "Thank God!"

Fred patted her arm. "There, there, Mother," he said gently.

"Don't you 'there, there' me, Fred Nesbitt. We should never have come to this God-forsaken country. Just think what might have happened to the child."

The adventure had ended happily, but the fun was over, and berry picking was ended for the day. They went back to the wagon in the clearing, prepared to leave for home "Next time I'll bring my gun," Ed Green said.

"Then you'll likely be shooting the rest of us, thinking we're bears," Mrs. Nesbitt responded drily.

She was thoroughly out of tune with the whole berry-picking expedition. Later on in the evening, though, when they were picking over the fruit, and the house was filled with the delicious scent of the jam-making, she softened a little.

"Maybe it was worth it, after all. This jam is going to taste pretty good when the snow flies." The others agreed heartily.

"It'll taste good before that, Mother," said Fred, licking his fingers.

"No you don't, Fred Nesbitt. This is all going to be put away, and not one spoonful gets eaten before there's snow on the ground."

After the raspberries, it was the time of the blueberries and saskatoons. The picking of the blueberries necessitated a trip to the bank of the North Saskatchewan River, and on this trip many of the Lloydminster people came too.

"What are these blueberries like?" Mrs. Nesbitt wanted to know. She was delighted to discover that they were quite familiar, being just the same as bilberries, or wimberries as they used to call them in Lancashire.

"They'll make good jam, too," she said, "but I'll let you all have a good feed of them first. Then we'll all have blue lips and teeth."

Saskatoons were new to them, except for the canned ones they had sampled at the farm on the way. They proved to be the best picking of all. You could get a pailful in no time, and, as Fred commented, you could stand right up to them, and not get a crick in your back.

Before the berry season was ended, every available tin, jar and bottle was filled with jam, and the children were already looking forward to the winter, so that they could begin tasting.

The Alberta Homesteader
a song from Alberta

1. My name is Dan Gold, an old bach'lor I am
   I'm keeping old batch on an elegant plan.
   You'll find me out here on Alberta's bush plain
   A-starving to death on a government claim.

2. So come to Alberta, there's room for you all
   Where the wind never ceases and the rain always falls,
   Where the sun always sets and there it remains
   Till we get frozen out on our government claims.

3. My house it is built of the natural soil,
   My walls are erected according to Hoyle,
   My roof has no pitch, it is level and plain,
   And I always get wet when it happens to rain.

4. My clothes are all ragged, my language is rough.
   My bread is case-hardened and solid and tough,
   My dishes are scattered all over the room,
   My floor gets afraid at the sight of a broom.

5. How happy I feel when I roll into bed,
   The rattlesnake rattles a tune at my head.
   The little mosquito devoid of all fear
   Crawls over my face and into my ear.

6. The little bed-bug so cheerful and bright,
   It keeps me up laughing two-thirds of the night,
   And the smart little flea with tacks in his toes
   Crawls up through my whiskers and tickles my nose.

Sarcastically

1. My name is Dan Gold, an old bach'-lor I am, I'm
keep-ing old batch on an e - le - gant plan. You'll find me out here on Al -
ber - ta's bush plain A - star-ving to death on a go-vern-ment claim.

7. You may try to raise wheat, you may try to raise rye,
   You may stay there and live, you may stay there and die,
   But as for myself, I'll no longer remain
   A-starving to death on a government claim.

8. So farewell to Alberta, farewell to the west,
   It's backwards I'll go to the girl I love best.
   I'll go back to the east and get me a wife
   And never eat cornbread the rest of my life.

The Bear That Thought He Was a Dog

by Sir Charles G. D. Roberts

The gaunt, black mother lifted her head from nuzzling happily at the velvet fur of her little one. The cub was but twenty-four hours old, and engrossed every emotion of her savage heart; but her ear had caught the sound of heavy footsteps coming up the mountain. They were confident, fearless footsteps, taking no care whatever to disguise themselves, so she knew at once that they were the steps of the only creature that presumed to go so noisily through the great silences. Her heart pounded with anxious suspicion. She gave the cub a reassuring lick, deftly set it aside with her great paws, and thrust her head forth cautiously from the door of the den.

She saw a man—a woodsman in brownish-grey homespuns and heavy leg-boots, and with a gun over his shoulder—slouching up along the faintly marked trail which led close past her doorway. Her own great tracks on the trail had been obliterated that morning by a soft and thawing fall of belated spring snow—"the robin snow," as it is called in New Brunswick—and the man, absorbed in picking his way by this unfamiliar route over the mountain, had no suspicion that he was in danger of trespassing. But the bear, with

80

that tiny black form at the bottom of the den filling her whole horizon, could not conceive that the man's approach had any other purpose than to rob her of her treasure. She ran back to the little one, nosed it gently into a corner, and anxiously pawed some dry leaves half over it. Then, her eyes aflame with rage and fear, she betook herself once more to the entrance, and crouched there motionless to await the coming of the enemy.

The man swung up the hill noisily, grunting now and again as his foothold slipped on the slushy, moss-covered stones. He fetched a huge breath of satisfaction as he gained a little strip of level ledge, perhaps a dozen feet in length, with a scrubby spruce bush growing at the other end of it. Behind the bush he made out what looked as if it might be the entrance to a little cave. Interested at once, he strode forward to examine it. At the first stride a towering black form, jaws agape and claws outstretched, crashed past the fir bush and hurled itself upon him.

A man brought up in the backwoods learns to think quickly, or, rather, to think and act in the same instant. Even as the great beast sprang, the man's gun leaped to its place and he fired. His charge was nothing more than heavy duck-shot, intended for some low-flying flock of migrant geese or brant. But at this close range, some seven or eight feet only, it tore through its target like a heavy mushroom bullet, and with a stopping force that halted the animal's charge in mid-air like the blow of a steam hammer. She fell in her tracks, a heap of huddled fur and grinning teeth.

"Gee," remarked the man, "that was a close call!" He ejected the empty shell and slipped in a fresh cartridge. Then he examined critically the warm heap of fur and teeth.

Perceiving that his victim was a mother, and also that her fur was rusty and ragged after the winter's sleep, sentiment and the sound utilitarianism of the backwoods stirred within him in a fine blend.

"Poor old beggar!" he muttered. "She must hev' a baby in yonder hole. That accounts for her kind of hasty ways. 'Most a pity

I had to shoot her jest now, when she's out o' season an' her pelt not worth the job of strippin' it!"

Entering the half darkness of the cave, he quickly discovered the cub in its ineffectual hiding-place. Young as it was, when he picked it up, it whimpered with terror and struck out with its baby paws, recognizing the smell of an enemy. The man grinned indulgently at this display of spirit.

"Gee, but ye're chock-full o' ginger!" said he. And then, being of an understanding heart and an experimental turn of mind, he laid the cub down and returned to the body of the mother. With his knife he cut off several big handfuls of the shaggy fur and stuffed it into his pockets. Then he rubbed his hands, his sleeves, and the breast of his coat on the warm body.

"There, now," said he, returning to the cave and once more picking up the little one, "I've made ye an orphant, to be sure, but I'm goin' to soothe yer feelin's all I kin. Ye must make believe as how I'm yer mammy till I kin find ye a better one."

Pillowed in the crook of his captor's arm, and with his nose snuggled into a bunch of his mother's fur, the cub ceased to wonder at a problem too hard for him, and dozed off into an uneasy sleep. And the man, pleased with his new plaything, went gently that he might not disturb its slumber.

Now it chanced that at Jabe Smith's farm, on the other side of the mountain, there had just been a humble tragedy. Jabe Smith's dog, a long-haired brown retriever, had been bereaved of her new-born puppies. Six of them she had borne, but five had been straightway taken from her and drowned; for Jabe, though compassionate of heart, had wisely decided that compassion would be too costly at the price of having his little clearing quite overrun with dogs. For two days, in her box in a corner of the dusky stable, the brown mother had wistfully poured out her tenderness upon the one remaining puppy; and then, when she had run into the house for a moment to snatch a bite of breakfast, one of Smith's big red oxen had strolled into the stable and blundered a great splay hoof into

the box. That had happened in the morning; and all day the brown mother had moped, whimpering and whining, about the stable, casting long distraught glances at the box in the corner, which she was unwilling either to approach or to quite forsake.

When her master returned, and came and looked in hesitatingly at the stable door, the brown mother saw the small furry shape in the crook of his arm. Her heart yearned to it at once. She fawned upon the man coaxingly, lifted herself with her forepaws upon his coat, and reached up till she could lick the sleeping cub. Somewhat puzzled, Jabe Smith went and looked into the box. Then he understood. "If you want the cub, Jinny, he's your'n all right. An' it saves me a heap o'bother."

Driven by his hunger, and reassured by the smell of the handful of fur which the woodsman left with him, the cub promptly accepted his adoption. She seemed very small, this new mother, and she had a disquieting odour; but the supreme thing, in the cub's eyes, was the fact she had something that assuaged his appetite. The flavour, to be sure, was something new, and novelty is a poor recommendation to babes of whatever kindred; but all the cub really asked of milk was that it should be warm and abundant. And soon, being assiduously licked and fondled, and nursed till his little belly was round as a melon, he forgot the cave on the mountainside and accepted Jabe Smith's barn as a quite normal abode for small bears.

Jinny was natively a good mother. Had her own pups been left to her, she would have lavished every care and tenderness upon them during the allotted span of weeks, and then, with inexorable decision, she would have weaned and put them away for their souls' good. But somewhere in her sturdy doggish make-up there was a touch of temperament, of something almost approaching imagination, to which this strange foster-child of hers appealed as no ordinary puppy could ever have done. She loved the cub with a certain extravagance, and gave herself up to it utterly. Even her beloved master fell into a secondary place, and his household, of which she had hitherto held herself the guardian, now seemed to her to exist merely for the benefit of this black prodigy which she imagined herself to have produced. The little one's astounding growth—for the cubs of the bear are born very small, and so must lose no time in making up arrears of stature—was an affair for which she took all credit to herself; and she never thought of weaning him till he himself decided the matter by preferring the solid dainties of the kitchen. When she could no longer nurse him, however, she remained his devoted comrade, playmate, satellite; and the cub, who was a roguish but amiable soul, repaid her devotion by imitating her in all ways possible. The bear being by nature a very silent animal, her noisy barking seemed always to stir his curiosity and admiration; but his attempts to imitate it resulted in nothing more than an occasional grunting *woof*. This throaty syllable, his only utterance besides the whimper which signalled the frequent demands of his appetite, came to be accepted as his name; and he speedily learned to respond to it.

Jabe Smith, as has been already pointed out, was a man of sympathetic discernment. In the course of no long time his discernment told him that Woof was growing up under the delusion that he was a dog. It was perhaps a convenience, in some ways, that he should not know he was a bear—he might be the more secure from troublesome ancestral suggestions. But as he appeared to claim all the privileges of his foster-mother, Jabe Smith's foreseeing eye considered the time, not far distant, when the sturdy and demonstrative little animal would grow to a giant of six or seven hundred pounds in weight, and still, no doubt, continue to think he was a dog. Jabe Smith began to discourage the demonstrativeness of Jinny, trusting her example would have the desired effect upon the cub. In particular, he set himself to remove from her mind any lingering notion that she would do for a lap-dog. He did not want any such notion as that to get itself established in Woof's young brain. Also, he broke poor Jinny at once of her affectionate habit of springing up and planting her forepaws upon his breast. That seemed to him a demonstration of ardour which, if practised by a seven-hundred-pound bear, might be a little overwhelming.

Jabe Smith had no children to complicate the situation. His family consisted merely of Mrs. Smith, a small but varying number of cats and kittens, Jinny, and Woof. Upon Mrs. Smith and the cats Woof's delusion came to have such effect that they, too, regarded him as a dog. The cats scratched him when he was little, and with equal confidence they scratched him when he was big. Mrs. Smith, as long as she was in good humour, allowed him the freedom of the house, coddled him with kitchen titbits, and laughed when his affectionate but awkward bulk got in the way of her outbursts of mopping or her paroxysms of sweeping. But when storm was in the air, she regarded him no more than a black poodle. At the heels of the more nimble Jinny, he would be chased in ignominy from the kitchen door, with Mrs. Jabe's angry broom thwacking at the spot where Nature had forgotten to give him a tail. At such times Jabe Smith was usually to be seen smoking contemplatively on the woodpile, and regarding the abashed fugitives with sympathy. This matter of a tail was one of the obstacles which Woof had to encounter in playing the part of a dog. He was indefatigable in his efforts to wag his tail. Finding no tail to wag, he did the best he could with his whole massive hind-quarters, to the discomfiture of all that got in the way. Yet, for all his clumsiness, his good will was so unchanging that none of the farmyard kindred had any dread of him, saving only the pig in his sty. The pig, being an incurable sceptic by nature, and, moreover, possessed of a keen and discriminating nose, persisted in believing him to be a bear and a lover of pork, and would squeal nervously at the sight of him. The rest of the farmyard folk accepted him at his own illusion, and appeared to regard him as a gigantic species of dog. And so, with nothing to mar his content but the occasional paroxysms of Mrs. Jabe's broom, Woof led the sheltered life and was glad to be a dog.

It was not until the autumn of his third year that Woof began to experience any discontent. Then, without knowing why, it seemed to him that there was something lacking in Jabe Smith's farmyard—even in Jabe Smith himself and in Jinny, his foster-mother. The smell of the deep woods beyond the pasture fields drew him strangely. He grew restless. Something called him; something stirred in his blood and would not let him be still. And one morning, when Jabe Smith came out in the first pink and amber of daybreak to fodder the horses, he found that Woof had disappeared. He was sorry, but he was not surprised. He tried to explain to the dejected Jinny that they would probably have the truant back again before long. But he was not adept in the language of dogs, and Jinny, failing for once to understand, remained disconsolate.

Once clear of the outermost stump pastures and burnt lands, Woof pushed on feverishly. The urge that drove him forward directed him toward the half-barren, rounded shoulders of old Sugar Loaf, where the blueberries at this season were ripe and bursting with juice. Here in the gold-green, windy open, belly-deep in the low, blue-jewelled bushes, Woof feasted greedily; but he felt it was not berries that he had come for.

When, however, he came upon a glossy young she-bear, her fine black muzzle bedaubed with berry juice, his eyes were opened to the object of his quest. Perhaps he thought she, too, was a dog; but, if so, she was in his eyes a dog of incomparable charm, more dear to him, though a new acquaintance, than even little brown Jinny, his kind mother, had ever been. The stranger, though at first somewhat puzzled by Woof's violent efforts to wag a nonexistent tail, apparently found her big wooer sympathetic. For the next few weeks, all through the golden, dreamy autumn of the New Brunswick woods, the two roamed together; and for the time Woof forgot the farm, his master, Jinny, and even Mrs. Jabe's impetuous broom.

But about the time of the first sharp frosts, when the ground was crisp with the new-fallen leaves, Woof and his mate began to lose interest in each other. She amiably forgot him and wandered off by herself, intent on nothing so much as satisfying her appetite, which had increased amazingly. It was necessary that she should load her ribs with fat to last her through her long winter's sleep in some cave or hollow tree. And as for Woof, once more he thought of Jabe Smith and Jinny, and the kind, familiar farmyard, and the delectable scraps from the kitchen, and the comforting smell of fried pancakes. What was the chill and lonely wilderness to him, a dog? He turned from grubbing up an ant stump and headed straight back for home.

When he got there, he found but a chimney standing naked and blackened over a tangle of charred ruins. A forest fire, some ten days back, had swept past that way, cutting a mile-wide swath through the woods and clean wiping out Jabe Smith's little homestead. It being too late in the year to begin rebuilding, the woodsman had betaken himself to the settlements for the winter, trusting to begin, in the spring, the slow repair of his fortunes.

Woof could not understand it at all. For a day he wandered disconsolately over and about the ruins, whining and sniffing, and filled with a sense of injury at being thus deserted. How glad he would have been to hear even the squeal of his enemy, the pig, or to feel the impetuous broom of Mrs. Jabe harassing his haunches! But even such poor consolation seemed to have passed beyond his ken. On the second day, being very hungry, he gave up all hope of bacon scraps, and set off to the woods to forage once more for himself.

As long as the actual winter held off, there was no great difficulty in this foraging. There were roots to be grubbed up, grubs, worms, and beetles, already sluggish with the cold, to be found under stones and logs, and ant-hills to be ravished. There were also the nests of bees and wasps, pungent but savoury. He was an expert in hunting the shy wood-mice, lying patiently in wait for them beside their holes and obliterating them, as they

came out, with a lightning stroke of his great paw. But when the hard frosts came, sealing up the moist turf under a crust of steel, and the snows, burying the mouse-holes under three or four feet of white fluff, then he was hard put to it for a living. Every day or two, in his distress, he would revisit the clearing and wander sorrowfully among the snow-clad ruins, hoping against hope that his vanished friends would presently return.

It was in one of the earliest of these melancholy visits that Woof first encountered a male of his own species, and showed how far he was from any consciousness of kinship. A yearling heifer of Jabe

Smith's, which had escaped from the fire and fled far into the wilderness, chanced to find her way back. For several weeks she had managed to keep alive on such dead grass as she could paw down to through the snow, and on such twigs of birch and poplar as she could manage to chew. Now, a mere ragged bag of bones, she stood in the snow behind the ruins, her eyes wild with hunger and despair.

Her piteous mooings caught the ear of a hungry old he-bear who was hunting in the woods near by. He came at once, hopefully. One stroke of his armed paw on the unhappy heifer's neck put a period to her pains, and the savage old prowler fell to his meal.

But, as it chanced, Woof also had heard, from a little further off, that lowing of the disconsolate heifer. To him it had come as a voice from the good old days of friendliness and plenty and impetuous brooms, and he had hastened toward the sound with new hope in his heart. He came just in time to see, from the edge of the clearing, the victim stricken down.

One lesson Woof had well learned from his foster-mother, and that was the obligation resting upon every honest dog to protect his master's property. The unfortunate heifer was undoubtedly the property of Jabe Smith. In fact, Woof knew her as a young beast who had often shaken her budding horns at him. Filled with righteous wrath, he rushed forward and hurled himself upon the slayer.

The latter was one of those morose old males, who, having forgotten or outgrown the comfortable custom of hibernation, are doomed to range the wilderness all winter. His temper, therefore, was raw enough in any case. At this flagrant interference with his own lawful kill, it flared to fury. His assailant was bigger than he, better nourished, and far stronger; but for some minutes he put up a fight which, for swift ferocity, almost daunted the hitherto unawakened spirit of Woof. A glancing blow of the stranger's, however, on the side of Woof's snout—only the remnant of a spent stroke, but enough to produce an effect on that most sensitive centre of a bear's dignity—and there was a sudden change in the conditions of the duel. Woof, for the first time in his life, saw red. It was a veritable berserk rage, this virgin outburst of his. His adversary simply went down like a rag baby before it, and was mauled to abject submission, in the smother of the snow, inside of half a minute. Feigning death, which, indeed, was no great feigning for him at that moment, he succeeded in deceiving the unsophisticated Woof, who drew back upon his haunches to consider his triumph. In that second the vanquished one writhed nimbly to his feet and slipped off apologetically through the snow. And Woof, placated by his victory, made no attempt to follow. The ignominies of Mrs. Jabe's broom were wiped out.

When Woof's elation had somewhat subsided, he laid himself down beside the carcass of the dead heifer. As the wind blew on that day, this corner of the ruins was a nook of shelter. Moreover, the body of the red heifer, dead and dilapidated though it was, formed in his mind a link with the happy past. It was Jabe Smith's property, and he got a certain comfort from lying beside it and guarding it for his master. As the day wore on, and his appetite grew more and more insistent, in an absent-minded way he began to gnaw at the good red meat beside him. At first, to be sure, this gave him a guilty conscience, and from time to time he would glance up nervously, as if apprehending the broom. But soon immunity brought confidence, his conscience ceased to trouble him, and the comfort derived from the nearness of the red heifer was increased exceedingly.

As long as the heifer lasted, Woof struck faithfully to his post as guardian, and longer, indeed. For nearly two days after the remains had quite disappeared—save for horns and hoofs and such bones as his jaws could not crush—he lingered. Then at last, urged by a ruthless hunger, and sorrowfully convinced that there was nothing more he could do for Jabe or Jabe for him, he set off again on his wanderings.

About three weeks later, forlorn of heart and exigent of belly,

Woof found himself in a part of the forest where he had never been before. But someone else had been there; before him was a broad trail, just such as Jabe Smith and his wood sled used to make. Here were the prints of horses' hooves. Woof's heart bounded hopefully. He hurried along down the trail. Then a faint, delectable savour, drawn across the sharp, still air, met his nostrils. Pork and beans—oh, assuredly! He paused for a second to sniff the fragrance again, and then lurched onwards at a rolling gallop. He rounded a turn of the trail, and there before him stood a logging camp.

To Woof a human habitation stood for friendliness and food and shelter. He approached, therefore, without hesitation.

There was no sign of life about the place, except for the smoke rising liberally from the stove-pipe chimney. The door was shut, but Woof knew that doors frequently opened if one scratched at them and whined persuasively. He tried it, then stopped to listen for an answer. The answer came—a heavy, comfortable snore from within the cabin. It was mid-morning, and the camp cook, having got his work done up, was sleeping in his bunk while the dinner was boiling.

Woof scratched and whined again. Then, growing impatient, he reared himself on his haunches in order to scratch with both paws at once. His luck favoured him, for he happened to scratch on the latch. It lifted, the door swung open suddenly, and he half fell across the threshold. He had not intended so abrupt an entrance, and he paused, peering with diffidence and hope into the homely gloom.

The snoring had stopped suddenly. At the rear of the cabin Woof made out a large, round, startled face, fringed with scanty red whiskers and a mop of red hair, staring at him from over the edge of an upper bunk. Woof had hoped to find Jabe Smith there. But this was a stranger, so he suppressed his impulse to rush in and wallow delightedly before the bunk. Instead of that, he came only half-way over the threshold, and stood there making those violent contortions which he believed to be wagging his tail.

To a cool observer of even the most limited intelligence it would have been clear that these contortions were intended to be conciliatory. But the cook of Conroy's Camp was taken by surprise, and he was not a cool observer—in fact, he was frightened. A gun was leaning against the wall below the bunk. A large, hairy hand stole forth, reached down and clutched the gun.

Woof wagged his haunches more coaxingly than ever, and took another hopeful step forward. Up went the gun. There was a blue-white spurt, and the report clashed deafeningly within the narrow quarters.

The cook was a poor shot at any time, and at this moment he was at a special disadvantage. The bullet went close over the top of Woof's head and sang waspishly across the clearing. Woof turned and looked over his shoulder to see what the man had fired at. If anything was hit, he wanted to go and get it and fetch it for the man, as Jabe and Jinny had taught him to do. But he could see no result of the shot. He whined deprecatingly and ventured all the way into the cabin.

The cook felt desperately for another cartridge. There was none to be found. He remembered that they were all in the chest by the door. He crouched back in the bunk, making himself as small as possible, and hoping that a certain hunk of bacon on the bench by the stove might divert the terrible stranger's attention and give him a chance to make a bolt for the door.

But Woof had not forgotten either the good example of Jinny or the discipline of Mrs. Jabe's broom. Far be it from him to help himself without leave. But he was very hungry. Something must be done to win the favour of the strangely unresponsive round-faced man in the bunk. Looking about him anxiously, he espied a pair of greasy cowhide "larrigans" lying on the floor near the door. Picking one up in his mouth, after the manner of his retriever foster-mother, he carried it over and laid it down, as a humble offering, beside the bunk.

Now, the cook, though he had been undeniably frightened, was by no means a fool. This touching gift of one of his own larrigans opened his eyes and his heart. Such a bear, he was assured, could harbour no evil intentions. He sat up in his bunk.

"Hullo!" said he. "What ye doin' here, sonny? What d'ye want o' me, anyhow?"

The huge black beast wagged his hind-quarters frantically and wallowed on the floor in his fawning delight at the sound of a human voice.

"Seems to think he's a kind of a dawg," muttered the cook thoughtfully. And then the light of certain remembered rumours broke upon his memory.

"I'll be jiggered," said he, "ef 'tain't that there tame b'ar Jabe Smith, over to East Fork, used to have afore he was burnt out!"

Climbing confidently from the bunk, he proceeded to pour a generous portion of molasses over the contents of the scrap pail, because he knew that bears had a sweet tooth. When the choppers and drivers came trooping in for dinner, they were somewhat taken aback to find a huge bear sleeping beside the stove. As the dangerous-looking slumberer seemed to be in the way—none of the men caring to sit too close to him—to their amazement the cook smacked the mighty hind-quarters with the flat of his hand, and bundled him unceremoniously into a corner. "'Pears to think he's some kind of a dawg," explained the cook, "so I let him come along in for company. He'll fetch yer larrigans an' socks an' things fer ye. An' it makes the camp a sight homier, havin' somethin' like a cat or a dawg about."

"Right you are!" agreed the boss. "But what was that noise we heard, along about an hour back? Did you shoot anything?"

"Oh, that was jest a little misunderstandin', before him an' me got acquainted," explained the cook, with a trace of embarrassment. "We made it up all right."

The Fire

by Susanna Moodie

Susanna Moodie and her husband and children suffered many hardships as English settlers on a wild Ontario bush farm. They struggled hard to make their wilderness homestead productive, despite bad weather, poor crops, and difficult neighbours. One day they almost lost all that they had worked so hard to gain.

The early part of the winter of 1837, a year never to be forgotten in the annals of Canadian history, was very severe. During the month of February, the thermometer often ranged from eighteen to twenty-seven degrees below zero.

The morning of the seventh was so intensely cold that everything liquid froze in the house. The wood that had been drawn for the fire was green, and it ignited too slowly to satisfy the shivering impatience of women and children; I grumbled over the wretched fire, at which I in vain endeavoured to thaw frozen bread, and to dress crying children.

It so happened that an old friend had been staying with us for a few days. She had left us for a visit to my sister, and as some relatives of hers were about to return to Britain, and had offered to convey letters to friends at home, I had been busy all the day before preparing a packet for England.

It was my intention to walk to my sister's with this packet, but the extreme cold of the morning had occasioned such delay, that it was late before the breakfast-things were cleared away.

After dressing, I found the air so keen that I could not venture out without some risk to my nose, and my husband kindly volunteered to go in my stead.

I had hired a young servant girl the day before. Her friends were only recently located in our vicinity, and she had never seen a stove until she came to our house. After Moodie left, I let the fire die away in the Franklin stove in the parlour, and went into the kitchen to prepare bread for the oven.

The girl, who was a good-natured creature, had heard me complain bitterly of the cold and the impossibility of getting the green wood to burn, and she thought that she would see if she could not make a good fire for me and the children, before my work was done. Without saying one word about her intention, she slipped out through a door that opened from the parlour into the garden, ran round to the woodyard, filled her lap with cedar chips, and, not knowing the nature of the stove, filled it entirely with the light wood.

Before I had the least idea of my danger, I was aroused from my task by the crackling and roaring of a large fire, and a suffocating smell of burning soot. I looked up at the kitchen cooking-stove. All was right there. I knew I had left no fire in the parlour stove; but not being able to account for the smoke and smell of burning, I opened the door, and, to my dismay, found the stove red-hot, from the front plate to the topmost pipe that let out the smoke through the roof.

My first impulse was to plunge a blanket snatched from the servant's bed, which stood in the kitchen, into cold water. This I thrust into the stove, and upon it I threw water, until all was cool below. I then ran up to the loft, and, by exhausting all the water in the house, even to that contained in the boilers upon the fire, tried to cool down the pipes which passed through the loft. I then sent the girl out of doors to look at the roof, which, as a very deep fall of snow had taken place the day before, I hoped would be completely covered, and safe from all danger of fire.

She quickly returned, stamping, and tearing her hair, and making a variety of uncouth outcries, from which I gathered that the roof was in flames.

This was terrible news, with my husband absent, no man in the house, and a mile and a quarter from any other habitation. I ran out to ascertain the extent of the misfortune, and found a large fire burning in the roof between the two stove pipes. The heat of the fires had melted off all the snow, and a spark from the burning pipe had already ignited the shingles. A ladder, which for several months had stood against the house, had been moved two days before to the barn, which was at the top of the hill near the road; there was no reaching the fire through that source. I got out the dining-table, and tried to throw water upon the roof by standing on a chair placed upon it, but I only expended a little water that remained in the boiler, without reaching the fire. The girl still continued weeping and lamenting.

"You must go for help," I said. "Run as fast as you can to my sister's, and fetch your master."

"And lave you, ma'arm, and the childher alone wid the burnin' house?"

"Yes, yes! Don't stay one moment."

"I have no shoes, ma'arm, and the snow is so deep."

"Put on your master's boots; make haste, or we shall be lost before help comes."

The girl put on the boots and started, shrieking "Fire!" the whole way. This was utterly useless, and only impeded her progress by exhausting her strength. After she had vanished from the head of the clearing into the wood, and I was left quite alone, with the house burning over my head, I paused one moment to reflect what had best be done.

The house was built of cedar logs; in all probability it would be consumed before any help could arrive. There was a brisk breeze blowing up from the frozen lake, and the thermometer stood at eighteen degrees below zero. We were placed between the two extremes of heat and cold, and there was as much danger from the one as the other. In the bewilderment of the moment the extent of the calamity never struck me; we needed but this to put the finishing stroke to our misfortunes, to be thrown naked, houseless, and penniless, upon the world. *"What shall I save first?"* was the thought just then uppermost in my mind. Bedding and clothing appeared the most essentially necessary, and, without another moment's pause, I set to work with a right good will to drag all that I could from my burning home.

While little Agnes, Dunbar, and baby Donald filled the air with their cries, Katie assisted me in carrying out sheets and blankets, and dragging trunks and boxes some way up the hill, to be out of the way of the burning brands when the roof should fall in.

How many anxious looks I gave to the head of the clearing as the fire increased, and large pieces of burning pine began to fall through the boarded ceiling about the lower rooms where we were at work. The children I had kept under a large dresser in the kitchen, but it now appeared absolutely necessary to remove them to a place of safety. To expose the young, tender things to the direful cold was almost as bad as leaving them to the mercy of the fire. At last I hit upon a plan to keep them from freezing. I emptied all the clothes out of a large, deep chest of drawers, and dragged the empty drawers up the hill; these I lined with blankets, and placed a child in each drawer, covering it well over with the bedding, giving to little Agnes the charge of the baby to hold between her knees, and keep well covered until help should arrive. Ah, how long it seemed coming!

The roof was now burning like a brush-heap, and, unconsciously, the child and I were working under a shelf upon which were deposited several pounds of gunpowder, which had been procured for blasting a well, as all our water had to be brought uphill from the lake. This gunpowder was in a stone jar, secured by a paper stopper; the shelf upon which it stood was on fire, but it was utterly forgotten by me at the time, and even afterwards, when my husband was working on the burning loft over it.

I found that I should not be able to take many more trips for goods. As I passed out of the parlour for the last time, Katie looked up at her father's flute, which was suspended upon two brackets, and said:

"Oh, dear mamma! do save papa's flute; he will be so sorry to lose it."

God bless the dear child for the thought! the flute was saved; and, as I succeeded in dragging out a heavy chest of clothes, and looked up once more despairingly to the road, I saw a man running at full speed. It was my husband. Help was at hand, and my heart uttered a deep thanksgiving as another and another figure came upon the scene.

I had not felt the intense cold, although without cap, or bonnet, or shawl, with my hands bare and exposed to the bitter biting air. The intense excitement, the anxiety to save all I could, had so totally diverted my thoughts from myself, that I had felt nothing of the danger to which I had been exposed; but now that help was near, my knees trembled under me, I felt giddy and faint, and dark shadows seemed dancing before my eyes.

The moment my husband and brother-in-law entered the house, the latter exclaimed:

"Moodie, the house is gone; save what you can of your winter stores and furniture."

Moodie thought differently. Prompt and energetic in danger, and possessing admirable presence of mind and coolness when others yield to agitation and despair, he sprang upon the burning loft and called for water. Alas, there was none!

"Snow, snow; hand me up pailfuls of snow!"

Oh! it was bitter work filling those pails with frozen snow; but Mr. T—and I worked at it as fast as we were able.

The violence of the fire was greatly checked by covering the boards of the loft with this snow. More help had now arrived. Young B— and S— had brought the ladder down with them from the barn, and were already cutting away the burning roof, and flinging the flaming brands into the deep snow.

"Mrs. Moodie, have you any pickled meat?"

"We have just killed one of our cows and salted it for winter stores."

"Well, then, fling the beef into the snow, and let us have the brine."

This was an admirable plan. Wherever the brine wetted the shingles, the fire turned from it, and concentrated into one spot.

But I had not time to watch the brave workers on the roof. I was fast yielding to the effects of over-excitement and fatigue, when my brother's team dashed down the clearing, bringing my excellent old friend, Miss B—, and the servant-girl.

My brother sprang out, carried me back into the house, and wrapped me up in one of the large blankets scattered about. In a few minutes I was seated with the dear children in the sleigh, and on the way to a place of warmth and safety.

Katie alone suffered from the intense cold. The dear little creature's feet were severely frozen, but were fortunately restored by her uncle discovering the fact before she approached the fire, and rubbing them well with snow.

In the meanwhile, the friends we had left so actively employed at the house, succeeded in getting the fire under before it had destroyed the walls. The only accident that occurred was to a poor dog that Moodie had called Snarleyowe. He was struck by a burning brand thrown from the house, and crept under the barn and died.

Beyond the damage done to the building, the loss of our potatoes and two sacks of flour, we had escaped in a manner

almost miraculous. This fact shows how much can be done by persons working in union, without bustle and confusion, or running in each other's way. Here were six men, who, without the aid of water, succeeded in saving a building, which, at first sight, almost all of them had deemed past hope. In after years, when entirely burnt out in a disastrous fire that consumed almost all we were worth in the world, some four hundred persons were present, with a fire-engine to second their endeavours, yet all was lost. Every person seemed in the way; and though the fire was discovered immediately after it took place, nothing was done beyond saving some of the furniture.

Our party was too large to be billeted upon one family. Mrs. T— took compassion upon Moodie, myself, and the baby, while their uncle received the three children to his hospitable home.

It was some weeks before Moodie succeeded in repairing the roof, the intense cold preventing anyone from working in such an exposed situation.

The news of our fire travelled far and wide. I was reported to have done prodigies and to have saved the greater part of our household goods before help arrived. Reduced to plain prose, these prodigies shrink into the simple and by no means marvellous fact, that during the excitement I dragged out chests which, under ordinary circumstances, I could not have moved; and that I was unconscious both of the cold and the danger to which I was exposed while working under a burning roof, which, had it fallen, would have buried both the children and myself under its ruins.

These circumstances appeared far more alarming, as all real danger does, after they were past. The fright and over-exertion gave my health a shock from which I did not recover for several months, and made me so fearful of fire, that from that hour it haunts me like a nightmare. Let the night be ever so serene, all stoves must be shut up, and the hot embers covered with ashes, before I dare retire to rest.

Jean Labadie's Big Black Dog

by Natalie Carlson

Once in another time, Jean Labadie was the most popular storyteller in the parish. He acted out every story so that it would seem more real.

When he told about the great falls of Niagara, he made a booming noise deep in his throat and whirled his fists around each other. Then each listener could plainly hear the falls and see the white water churning and splashing as if it were about to pour down on his own head. But Jean Labadie had to stop telling his stories about the *loup-garou,* that demon who takes the shape of a terrible animal and pounces upon those foolish people who go out alone at night. Every time the storyteller dropped down on all fours, rolled his eyes, snorted, and clawed at the floor, his listeners ran away from him in terror.

It was only on the long winter evenings that Jean had time to tell these tales. All the rest of the year, he worked hard with his cows and his pigs and his chickens.

One day Jean Labadie noticed that his flock of chickens was

getting smaller and smaller. He began to suspect that his neighbour, André Drouillard, was stealing them. Yet he never could catch André in the act.

For three nights running, Jean took his gun down from the wall and slept in the henhouse with his chickens. But the only thing that happened was that his hens were disturbed by having their feeder roost with them, and they stopped laying well. So Jean sighed and put his gun back and climbed into his own bed again.

One afternoon when Jean went to help his neighbour mow the weeds around his barn, he found a bunch of grey chicken feathers near the fence. Now he was sure that André was taking his chickens, for all of his neighbour's chickens were scrawny white things.

He did not know how to broach the matter to André without making an enemy of him. And when one lives in the country and needs help with many tasks, it is a great mistake to make an enemy of a close neighbour. Jean studied the matter as his scythe went swish, swish through the tall weeds. At last he thought of a way out.

"Have you seen my big black dog, André?" he asked his neighbour.

"What big black dog?" asked André. "I didn't know you had a dog."

"I just got him from the Indians," said Jean. "Someone has been stealing my chickens so I got myself a dog to protect them. He is a very fierce dog, bigger than a wolf and twice as wild."

Jean took one hand off the scythe and pointed to the ridge behind the barn.

"There he goes now," he cried, "with his big red tongue hanging out of his mouth. See him!"

André looked but could see nothing.

"Surely you must see him. He runs along so fast. He lifts one paw this way and another paw that way."

As Jean said this, he dropped the scythe and lifted first one hand

in its black glove and then the other.

André looked at the black gloves going up and down like the paws of a big black dog. Then he looked toward the ridge. He grew excited.

"Yes, yes," he cried, "I do see him now. He is running along the fence. He lifts one paw this way and another paw that way, just like you say."

Jean was pleased that he was such a good actor he could make André see a dog that didn't exist at all.

"Now that you have seen him," he said, "you will know him if you should meet. Give him a wide path and don't do anything that will make him suspicious. He is a very fierce watchdog."

André promised to stay a safe distance from the big black dog.

Jean Labadie was proud of himself over the success of his trick. No more chickens disappeared. It seemed that his problem was solved.

Then one day André greeted him with, "I saw your big black dog in the road today. He was running along lifting one paw this way and another paw that way. I got out of his way, you can bet my life!"

Jean Labadie was pleased and annoyed at the same time. Pleased that André believed so completely in the big black dog that he actually could see him. He was also annoyed because the big black dog had been running down the road when he should have been on the farm.

Another day André leaned over the fence.

"Good day, Jean Labadie," he said. "I saw your big black dog on the other side of the village. He was jumping over fences and bushes. Isn't it a bad thing for him to wander so far away? Someone might take him for the *loup-garou.*"

Jean Labadie was disgusted with his neighbour's good imagination.

"André," he asked, "how can my dog be on the other side of the village when he is right here at home? See him walking through

108

the yard, lifting one paw this way and another paw that way?"

André looked in Jean's yard with surprise.

"And so he is," he agreed. "My faith, what a one he is! He must run like lightning to get home so fast. Perhaps you should chain him up. Someone will surely mistake such a fast dog for the *loup-garou*."

Jean shrugged hopelessly.

"All right," he said. "Perhaps you are right. I will chain him near the henhouse."

"They will be very happy to hear that in the village," said André. "Everyone is afraid of him. I have told them all about him, how big and fierce he is, how his long red tongue hangs out of his mouth and how he lifts one paw this way and another paw that way."

Jean was angry.

"I would thank you to leave my dog alone, André Drouillard," he said stiffly.

"Oh, ho, and that I do!" retorted André. "But today on the road he growled and snapped at me. I would not be here to tell the story if I hadn't taken to a tall maple tree."

Jean Labadie pressed his lips together.

"Then I will chain him up this very moment." He gave a long low whistle. "Come, fellow! Here, fellow!"

André Drouillard took to his heels.

Of course, this should have ended the matter, and Jean Labadie thought that it had. But one day when he went to the village to buy some nails for his roof, he ran into Madame Villeneuve in a great how-does-it-make of excitement.

"Jean Labadie," she cried to him, "you should be ashamed of yourself, letting that fierce dog run loose in the village."

"But my dog is chained up in the yard at home," said Jean.

"So André Drouillard told me," said Madame, "but he has broken loose. He is running along lifting one paw this way and another paw that way, with the broken chain dragging in the dust. He growled at me and bared his fangs. It's a lucky thing his chain caught on a bush or I would not be talking to you now."

Jean sighed.

"Perhaps I should get rid of my big black dog," he said. "Tomorrow I will take him back to the Indians."

So next day Jean hitched his horse to the cart and waited until he saw André Drouillard at work in his garden. Then he whistled loudly toward the yard, made a great show of helping his dog climb up between the wheels and drove past André's house with one arm curved out in a bow, as if it were around the dog's neck.

"*Au revoir*, André!" he called. Then he looked at the empty half of the seat. "Bark good-bye to André Drouillard, fellow, for you are leaving here forever."

Jean drove out to the Indian village and spent the day with his friends, eating and talking. It seemed a bad waste of time when there was so much to be done on the farm, but on the other hand, it was worth idling all day in order to end the big black dog matter.

Dusk was falling as he rounded the curve near his home. He saw the shadowy figure of André Drouillard waiting for him near his gate. A feeling of foreboding came over Jean.

"What is it?" he asked his neighbour. "Do you have some bad news for me?"

"It's about your big black dog," said André. "He has come back home. Indeed he beat you by an hour. It was that long ago I saw him running down the road to your house with his big red tongue hanging out of his mouth and lifting one paw this way and another paw that way."

Jean was filled with rage. For a twist of tobacco, he would have struck André with his horsewhip.

"André Drouillard," he shouted, "you are a liar! I just left the big black dog with the Indians. They have tied him up."

André sneered.

"A liar am I? We shall see who is the liar. Wait until the others see your big black dog running around again."

So Jean might as well have accused André of being a chicken

110

thief in the first place, for now they were enemies anyway. And he certainly might as well have stayed home and fixed his roof.

Things turned out as his neighbour had hinted. Madame Villeneuve saw the big black dog running behind her house. Henri Dupuis saw him running around the corner of the store. Delphine Langlois even saw him running through the graveyard among the tombstones. And always as he ran along, he lifted one paw this way and another paw that way.

There came that day when Jean Labadie left his neighbour chopping wood all by himself, because they were no longer friends, and drove into the village to have his black mare shod. While he was sitting in front of the blacksmith shop, André Drouillard came galloping up at a great speed. He could scarcely hold the reins, for one hand was cut and bleeding.

A crowd quickly gathered.

"What is wrong, André Douillard?" they asked.

"Have you cut yourself?"

"Where is Dr. Brisson? Someone fetch Dr. Brisson."

André Drouillard pointed his bleeding hand at Jean Labadie.

"His big black dog bit me," he accused. "Without warning, he jumped the fence as soon as Jean drove away and sank his teeth into my hand."

There was a gasp of horror from every throat. Jean Labadie reddened. He walked over to André and stared at the wound.

"It looks like an axe cut to me," he said.

Then everyone grew angry at Jean Labadie and his big black dog. They threatened to drive them both out of the parish.

"My friends," said Jean wearily, "I think it is time for this matter to be ended. The truth of it is that I have no big black dog. I never had a big black dog. It was all a joke."

"Aha!" cried André. "Now he is trying to crawl out of the blame. He says he has no big black dog. Yet I have seen it with my own eyes, running around and lifting one paw this way and another paw that way."

"I have seen it, too," cried Madame Villeneuve. "It ran up and growled at me."

"And I."

"And I."

Jean Labadie bowed his head.

"All right, my friends," he said. "There is nothing more I can do about it. I guess that big black dog will eat me out of house and home for the rest of my life."

"You mean you won't make things right about this hand?" demanded André Drouillard.

"What do you want me to do?" asked Jean.

"I will be laid up for a week at least," said André Drouillard, "and right at harvest time. Then, too, there may be a scar. But for two of your plumpest pullets, I am willing to overlook the matter and be friends again."

"That is fair," cried Henri Dupuis.

"It is just," cried the blacksmith.

"A generous proposal," agreed everyone.

"And now we will return to my farm," said Jean Labadie, "and I will give André two of my pullets. But all of you must come. I want witnesses."

A crowd trooped down the road to watch the transaction. It was almost as large as the one that had attended Tante Odette's skunk party.

After Jean had given his neighbour two of his best pullets, he commanded the crowd, "Wait!"

He went into the house. When he returned, he was carrying his gun.

"I want witnesses," explained Jean, "because I am going to shoot my big black dog. I want everyone to see this happen."

The crowd murmured and surged. Jean gave a long low whistle toward the henhouse.

"Here comes my big black dog," he pointed. "You can see how he runs to me with his big red tongue hanging out and lifting one

paw this way and another paw that way."

Everyone saw the big black dog.

Jean Labadie lifted his gun to his shoulder, pointed it at nothing and pulled the trigger. There was a deafening roar and the gun kicked Jean to the ground. He arose and brushed off his blouse. Madame Villeneuve screamed and Delphine Langlois fainted.

"There," said Jean, brushing away a tear, "it is done. That is the end of my big black dog. Isn't that true?"

And everyone agreed that the dog was gone for good.

So remember this, my friends: If you must make up a big black dog, do not allow others to help or you may find that you are no longer the dog's master.

Midnight
by Archibald Lampman

From where I sit, I see the stars,
　　And down the chilly floor
The moon between the frozen bars
　　Is glimmering dim and hoar.

Without in many a peakèd mound
　　The glinting snowdrifts lie;
There is no voice or living sound;
　　The embers slowly die.

Yet some wild thing is in mine ear;
　　I hold my breath and hark;
Out of the depth I seem to hear
　　A crying in the dark:

No sound of man or wife or child,
　　No sound of beast that groans,
Or of the wind that whistles wild,
　　Or of the tree that moans:

I know not what it is I hear;
　　I bend my head and hark:
I cannot drive it from mine ear,
　　That crying in the dark.

Riel's Farewell

a song from Saskatchewan

1. I send this letter to you
   To tell my grief and pain,
   And as I lie imprisoned
   I long to see again
   You, my beloved mother,
   And all my comrades dear,
   I write these words in my heart's blood:
   No ink or pen is here.

2. My friends in arms and children,
   Please weep and pray for me.
   I fought hard for our country
   So that we might be free.
   When you receive this letter
   Please weep for me and pray
   That I may die with bravery
   Upon that fearful day.

This song was sung to Barbara Cass-Beggs by Joseph Gaspard Jeannotte, an old Métis living at Lebret, Saskatchewan, who said that it had been composed by Louis Riel during his last days when Riel was imprisoned in Regina after his Métis followers were defeated. Riel was tried and sentenced to death and, despite the protests of French-Canadians, he was hanged at Regina on November 16, 1885.

The White Owl

by Hazel Boswell

It was a still day late in September. The maples were glowing scarlet and gold; the ploughing had been done, and the fields lay bare and brown under the silver grey sky. Madame Blais sat on an upturned box on the narrow gallery that ran the length of the summer kitchen. She was plaiting long strings of red onions to hang in the attic for the winter. The little gallery was heaped with vegetables: great golden yellow squashes, green pumpkins, creamy brown turnips, and great piles of green cabbages and glossy red carrots.

It was a good day for work. Her husband, and Joseph her eldest boy, together with their neighbour, Exdras Boulay, had gone off to repair the old sugar *cabane*. Her sister's fiancé, Felix Leroy, who had come up from the States for a holiday, had gone with them. Not to work. He despised that sort of work, for he was a factory hand in the United States and, as he said, "made more money in a week than he would make in a month working on the land." The older children were off at school; the little ones, Gaetané, Jean-Paul, and Marie-Ange, were playing happily with old "Puppay." Me'Mère was spinning in the kitchen keeping an eye on P'tit Charles who was sleeping peacefully in his cradle.

Madame worked happily. She didn't often get such a good day for work. Her mind was turning in a placid, peaceful circle, "Que tous s'adone bien aujourd-hui."

Suddenly the peace was broken. Puppay had begun to bark furiously; then the barking changed to joyful yapping. The children were shouting too. Madame turned on her box and looked out to where they had been playing, but they had left their game and were racing off across the field. As her eye followed them on the far side of the field she saw her husband, Joseph, and Exdras Boulay coming out of the wood by the road to the old sugar cabane.

Me'Mère had heard the noise too and had come to the door. "What is it?" she asked, "Un Jerusalem?" "No," answered Madame, "it's the men coming home, and it's not yet four. Something must have happened."

She watched the men anxiously as they crossed the field. She noticed that Felix wasn't with them. As they came up to the house she called out, "What has happened?"

No one answered her; the men tramped on in silence. When they got to the house, her husband sat down on the step of the gallery and began taking off his *bottes-sauvages*. The other two and the children stood watching him.

"Where is Felix?" asked Madame.

"He wouldn't come with us."

"Why did you leave so early?"

Again there was silence; then her husband said, "We saw the Hibou Blanc."

"You saw him?"

"Yes," answered her husband, "that's why we came home."

"Why didn't Felix come with you?"

"He said it was all nonsense. Old men's stories."

"You should have made him come with you," said Me'Mère. "You can't remember the last time the Hibou Blanc came. But I can. It was just two years after I was married. Bonté Lemay was

119

like Felix, he didn't believe. He stayed on ploughing when the others left. The horse got scared and ran away. Bonté's arm was caught in the reins and he was dragged after the plough. His head struck a stone and he was dead when they found him. His poor mother. How she cried. One doesn't make fun of the Hibou Blanc."

The noise had wakened P'tit Charles and he began to cry. Madame went in to the kitchen and picked him up. She felt to see if he was wet; and then sat down by the stove, and began to feed him. The men came in too and sat around in the kitchen.

"Do you think Felix will have the sense to come home?" asked Madame.

Joseph shook his head and spat skilfully into the brown earthenware spittoon.

"No fear," he answered. "He says in the States they have more sense than to believe all those old stories."

"If Felix stays on in the woods, harm will certainly come to him," said Me'Mère, "I tell you the Hibou Blanc always brings disaster."

"Why don't you go and speak to the Curé?" said Madame Blais.

"He's away at Rimouski for a retreat," answered Exdras. "I saw his housekeeper, Philomène, yesterday, and she told me. They had sent for him to bring the last rites to old Audet Lemay who was dying, but he was away and they had to send for the Curé of St. Anselem instead."

"Well, it's time to get the cows," said Monsieur Blais. "Go along and get them, Joseph."

Joseph got up and went out. The children and Puppay joined him.

Me'Mère went back to her spinning. Madame Blais put P'tit Charles back in his cradle, then went off to milk the cows. There were ten cows to milk. Her husband and Joseph did the milking with her and up to a year before Me'Mère had always helped too.

120

The autumn evenings close in quickly in the north. By the time the cows were milked and supper finished, the clear cold green of evening had swept up over the sky; the stars were out, and the little silver crescent of the moon had risen over the maple wood. Joseph was sitting out on the step of the little gallery, his eyes fastened on the break in the maple wood that marked the road leading to the sugar cabin. Every now and then his father went out and joined him. They were both watching for Felix.

As the kitchen clock began to strike eight Madame put down her work. "It's time for the Rosary," she said. "Tell Joseph to come in." Her husband opened the door and called to Joseph. He came in, followed by Puppay.

The family pulled their chairs up round the stove, for the evenings were beginning to be chilly, and it was cold away from the stove.

Me'Mère began the Rosary: "*Je crois en Dieu, le Père tout-puissant. . . .*" The quiet murmur of their voices filled the kitchen.

When the Rosary was said Madame sent the children off to bed. Then she went to the salon and got a *cierge bénit,* lit it, and put it in the kitchen window. "May God have pity on him," she said. Then she picked up P'tit Charles and went off to bed with her husband, while Me'Mère went to her little room next to the salon.

It was bright and cold the next day, and the ground was covered with white hoar-frost.

Joseph was the first to speak of Felix. "He may have gone and slept with one of the neighbours," he said.

"If he did he'd be back by now," answered his father.

They were still eating their breakfast when Exdras Boulay came into the kitchen.

"Felix hasn't come back?" he asked.

Before anyone could answer, the door opened and two other neighbours came in. The news of Felix and the Hibou Blanc had

122

already spread along the road. Soon there were eight men and boys in the kitchen and half a dozen excited children.

The men sat round in the kitchen smoking. Old Alphonse Ouellet did most of the talking. He was always the leader in the parish.

"We'll have to go and find him," he said.

"It's too bad the Curé isn't here to come with us. Well, we might as well start off now. Bring your rosary with you," he told Monsieur Blais.

Madame Blais and Me'Mère and a group of the children stood on the kitchen gallery watching the men as they tramped off along the rough track to the maple wood.

"May God have them in His care," said Madame.

"And may He have pity on Felix," added Me'Mère, and she crossed herself.

In the maple wood the ground was still covered with frost. Every little hummock of fallen leaves was white with it, and the puddles along the track were frozen solid. The men walked in silence. A secret fear gripped each one of them that they might suddenly see the Hibou Blanc perched on some old stump, or one of the snow-covered hummocks. A few hundred yards from the sugar cabin they found Felix. He was lying on his back. His red shirt looked at first like a patch of red maple leaves lying in the hoar-frost. A great birch had fallen across his chest, pinning him to the ground. One of his hands was grasping a curl of the bark—his last mad effort to try and free himself.

The men stood round staring down at him, the immense silence of the woods surrounding them. Then from far away in the distance came a thin whinnying note, the shrill triumphant cry of *Le Hibou Blanc*.

The Cremation of Sam McGee
by Robert Service

There are strange things done in the midnight sun
  By the men who moil for gold;
The Arctic trails have their secret tales
  That would make your blood run cold;
The Northern Lights have seen queer sights,
  But the queerest they ever did see
Was that night on the marge of Lake Lebarge
  I cremated Sam McGee.

Now Sam McGee was from Tennessee, where
  the cotton blooms and blows.
Why he left his home in the South to roam
  round the Pole God only knows.
He was always cold, but the land of gold
  seemed to hold him like a spell;
Though he'd often say in his homely way that
  he'd "sooner live in hell."

On a Christmas Day we were mushing our way
  over the Dawson trail.
Talk of your cold! through the parka's fold it
  stabbed like a driven nail.
If our eyes we'd close, then the lashes froze,
  till sometimes we couldn't see;
It wasn't much fun, but the only one to
  whimper was Sam McGee.

And that very night as we lay packed tight in
    our robes beneath the snow,
And the dogs were fed, and the stars o'erhead
    were dancing heel and toe,
He turned to me, and, "Cap," says he, "I'll
    cash in this trip, I guess;
And if I do, I'm asking that you won't refuse
    my last request."

Well, he seemed so low that I couldn't say no;
    then he says with a sort of moan:
"It's the cursed cold, and it's got right hold
    till I'm chilled clean through to the bone.
Yet 'taint being dead, it's my awful dread of
    the icy grave that pains;
So I want you to swear that, foul or fair, you'll
    cremate my last remains."

A pal's last need is a thing to heed, so I swore I
    would not fail;
And we started on at the streak of dawn, but
    God! he looked ghastly pale.
He crouched on the sleigh, and he raved all
    day of his home in Tennessee;
And before nightfall a corpse was all that was
    left of Sam McGee.

There wasn't a breath in that land of death,
    and I hurried, horror driven,
With a corpse half-hid that I couldn't get rid,
    because of a promise given;
It was lashed to the sleigh, and it seemed to say:
    "You may tax your brawn and brains,
But you promised true, and it's up to you to
    cremate those last remains."

Now a promise made is a debt unpaid, and the
　　trail has its own stern code.
In the days to come, though my lips were
　　dumb, in my heart how I cursed that load.
In the long, long night, by the lone firelight,
　　while the huskies, round in a ring.
Howled out their woes to the homeless snows—
　　O God! how I loathed the thing.

And every day that quiet clay seemed to heavy
　　and heavier grow;
And on I went, though the dogs were spent
　　and the grub was getting low;
The trail was bad, and I felt half mad, but I
　　swore I would not give in;
And I'd often sing to the hateful thing, and it
　　hearkened with a grin.

Till I came to the marge of Lake Lebarge, and
　　a derelict there lay;
It was jammed in the ice, but I saw in a trice
　　it was called the "Alice May."
And I looked at it, and I thought a bit, and I
　　looked at my frozen chum:
Then, "Here," said I, with a sudden cry, "is
　　my cre-ma-tor-ium."

Some planks I tore from the cabin floor, and I
　　lit the boiler fire;
Some coal I found that was lying around, and I
　　heaped the fuel higher;
The flames just soared, and the furnace roared
　　—such a blaze you seldom see;
And I burrowed a hole in the glowing coal, and
　　I stuffed in Sam McGee.

Then I made a hike, for I didn't like to hear
   him sizzle so;
And the heavens scowled, and the huskies
   howled, and the wind began to blow.
It was icy cold, but the hot sweat rolled down
   my cheeks, and I don't know why;
And the greasy smoke in an inky cloak went
   streaking down the sky.

I do not know how long in the snow I wrestled
   with grisly fear;
But the stars came out and they danced about
   ere again I ventured near;
I was sick with dread, but I bravely said: "I'll
   just take a peep inside.
I guess he's cooked, and it's time I looked,"
   . . . then the door I opened wide.

And there sat Sam, looking cool and calm, in
   the heart of the furnace roar;
And he wore a smile you could see a mile, and
   he said: "Please close that door.
It's fine in here, but I greatly fear you'll let in
   the cold and storm—
Since I left Plumtree, down in Tennessee, it's
   the first time I've been warm."

There are strange things done in the midnight sun
   By the men who moil for gold;
The Arctic trails have their secret tales
   That would make your blood run cold;
The Northern Lights have seen queer sights,
   But the queerest they ever did see
Was that night on the marge of Lake Lebarge
   I cremated Sam McGee.

Mosaic

The North Wind
by Joanne Lysyk

Once, when I was young I knew the wind.
I called "Wi-ind, North Wi-ind"
And it came,
   tramping the grass so that it lay flat,
And whinnyed high and shrill like a whistle.
I saddled it with imagination,
   and bridled it with dreams.

And I got on and we went, and the trees
   bowed down in our passing.
I was exhilarated with the speed
   and lay down on his neck to keep
   balance,
And his snowy mane whipped about my face.
His unshod hoofs made no sound
   as he trod on the stars.
His breath made icicles on the houses
   we passed
And then he bucked.

"Panther Cubs"

from *Panther* by Roderick Haig-Brown

*A panther's life on the plateaux of Vancouver Island is a dangerous one.
Blackstreak, a vigorous male, has been shot, but a new and stronger
hunter will be born—his son Ki-yu.*

Blackstreak had travelled down the Storm River towards death.
But when Nassa turned down the Wapiti as the first snow fell on
the Heather Plateau, she bore life within her—Blackstreak's life.

It was with her as the snow-line crept farther and farther down
the slopes of the high hills, as the deer moved slowly down and
she followed them; with her all the while she killed and fed and
roamed. It drove her to hunt more skilfully, to kill more
frequently, to guard herself more carefully against weakness and
fatigue. It even drove her, through an instinct that had survived
generations of comparative security, to forsake her usual winter
range around Wolverine Lake and travel farther down towards
the coast, into country that the wolves only find when the snow
is very deep in the hills.

It quickened within her as she came to the great bend in the river below Wapiti Lake, and urged her to search among thickets and mazes of windfalls until she found a dry, warm place beneath the up-torn root of a great Douglas fir. Here she settled herself, for the lives within her were heavy. In a little while she slipped them from her, three lives, tiny and blind and mewing. The night after her cubs were born she went out and killed a yearling doe, barely a hundred yards away from the big root.

It was late in December, about five months after she had been with Blackstreak on the Plateau, when Nassa began to suckle her cubs. For fourteen days they remained blind, then they opened misty, slate-blue eyes and began to take note of their small world. It was a good world. Their mother's body was with them nearly all the time, and it provided food and warmth. When it was not with them they were cold and miserable, so they huddled together beneath the root, each one fighting for a place between the other two.

But Nassa cared little enough about leaving them, even after their eyes were open. She had to kill often—sometimes twice within a week—to keep up her strength, but hunting was easy and she roamed but little. She loved to lie on her side under the root and offer her milk to the cubs; she loved to feel their struggles to reach her when she first lay down, to hear them pawing at one another and mewing until at last each found what it wanted and settled to gorge itself, tiny paws working rhythmically against her udder, tiny stomachs swelling almost visibly to rounded tightness, tiny voices grunting with eagerness, then purring satisfaction.

They grew quickly. At four weeks they were over a foot long from their pink nostrils to the pointed tips of their long, barred tails. Their bodies were a pale tawny colour, marked all over with great dark brown spots, spots that were almost perfect circles. Their paws and fore-legs seemed disproportionately broad and heavy, and one of the three, the only male, was already slightly larger and stronger than the other two. Sometimes, sitting up peacefully, contented or curious, they seemed harmless, pretty little things, far more attractive to watch than the prettiest of domestic kittens. But if anything frightened or disturbed them they instantly became tiny furies, backing away, paws raised ready to strike, ears laid flat back against their skulls, snarling and hissing. And even in repose, even in clumsy play, they had a dignity that is not to be found in ordinary kittens. The smooth rhythm of their miniature yet powerful muscles; the savage black patches, sprouting long white whiskers from either side of strangely wise and confident faces—these were strong, menacing, definite things, even in such tiny, utterly dependent creatures.

Nassa had chosen her place well, but she was not quite without worries during those first weeks. A lone wolf was following her, living upon the remains of her kills. She despised the wolf, and he had no wish to meet her face to face, but she feared him for her cubs and dared not leave them long in case he should happen upon them. And whenever she returned to them after feeding she circled and doubled and waited on her tracks to make sure that she was not followed.

Not until two or three weeks after the cubs had first opened their eyes did she begin to roam at all widely again, and then she nearly always travelled at night, making a vague, irregular circle, two or three miles in diameter. Beside Blackstreak she had seemed a slender, light, graceful thing, yet she was really a mass of tremendously powerful muscles and tendons and sinews, all of which had to be working efficiently if she was to live, all of which had to be exercised if they were to work efficiently. So, at times, the urge to roam was stronger upon her than the urge to be with her cubs. But her thoughts were never far from the cubs and no matter where she happened to be, near them or far away, up-wind of them or down-wind, in strange country or familiar country, she could always go back to them by the straightest of straight lines if she so wished. And often a sudden intuitive

anxiety drove her back—only to find the cubs exactly as she had left them, huddled together beneath the sheltering root.

Fortunately there was little snow that winter and few hunters were tempted out, even by the bounty of forty dollars that the government offered on the hide of any and every panther over the age of two weeks. David Milton had returned to his home near the mouth of the Wapiti after the death of King, and he also went out into the woods less frequently than usual that year, though he hunted a good deal along the streams that flow into the Wapiti below the big bend. So Nassa saw neither dogs nor men near her precious patch of windfalls, and in time she even ceased to worry a great deal about the wolf—he was a scavenger, a hanger-on, a snapper-up of bones and pieces of hide and hair and entrails with which she would never have concerned herself. And the cubs were growing stronger, more able to hide themselves from any danger that threatened them while she was away.

When they were about a month old the cubs began to realize that there was a far bigger world than the patch of dry earth beneath the shelter of the big fir root. Ki-yu, the male, was the most definite and determined of the three. He had always been the first to settle himself to his mother's udder, always the last to leave it when his stomach could hold no more. Now he was the first to crawl out from the shelter of the root and gaze insolently upon the outside world of tangled forest and piled windfalls.

But it was a bad moment for the first venture, for his mother returned silently from nowhere almost as he settled himself on his haunches, picked him up gently by the loose fur of his back and carried him down under the root again. He hissed and swore at her, but he was contented enough to be with her—and determined enough to crawl out again as soon as she next left them.

This time he had the world to himself, so he sat down to examine it, ears cocked, tongue darting out now and then to lick

136

his nose appreciatively. Soon the other two cubs came out and sat near him, and soon it was not enough to sit there and admire. One had to travel and touch, to explore and climb and experiment.

Within three or four yards of the root were many strange and wonderful things. A leaf that crackled underfoot and had to be subdued with a snarl and a mighty paw-stroke; a piece of moss that waved gently on a low-hanging limb until pounced upon and torn from its place; another limb, into which one backed when fighting with the moss and which instantly became a menace, to be faced by a tremendous bound, all four feet off the ground at once, and a prodigious turn. It was all good.

Then a blue jay, coming on silent wings from silence, scolded rudely, raucously; so it was time to snarl vicious, half-frightened little snarls and back away. The blue jay hopped and fluttered twenty feet nearer; more snarls and little growls. Ki-yu wouldn't back away any more. He opened his mouth and spat, and his ears lay flat. His whole face became a mask of rage and his grey-blue eyes flashed terrifying threats. But the blue jay only laughed and flew up on to a log.

Nassa found them all three curled peacefully together under the root when she came back, but she knew they had been outside and seemed to accept it quietly enough from then on; they had been out and were safe; they would go out again and return safely again. So they learned to play in and out among the windfalls, to climb a little and chase one another, to fall safely, to jump and lope and spring, always balancing themselves with the swing of their long tails. Playing and climbing began to build their muscles, taught them the use of claws and teeth, something of the use of eyes and ears and nose.

One day the three of them had climbed on to the big fir and were playing along the trunk. Ki-yu chased one sister, caught her and rolled her over on her back. The other sister galloped clumsily down the log after him, her whole attention centred upon the exact spot on his tail that she would bite when she reached him. But something distracted her before she reached him. Her gallop changed abruptly to a slow, stiff walk and she stared ahead of her, searching among criss-crossed windfalls for she knew not what. Suddenly she found it, stopped sharply and crouched back. A strange, full-grown panther was standing a little way off, motionless, head raised, fore-paws set on a fallen tree, watching the cubs. A moment later the other little female stopped fighting Ki-yu and looked backwards from where she was lying. She too saw the strange panther. Ki-yu continued his attack upon her throat for a moment, then found her unresisting, sensed that something was amiss and looked up. For a moment all three cubs were motionless, then Ki-yu backed away suspiciously. The first little female rolled over and crouched. The other one was still crouching, glaring. Ki-yu stood and glared also.

The strange panther watched all their movements. She seemed fascinated by the cubs, curious about them, but in no way hostile. Suddenly she moved her head, looked past them and snarled. Ki-yu spat; his two sisters opened their jaws and hissed. Then a red shape hurled past them. The strange female turned and leapt away, with Nassa bounding close behind her. Ki-yu and his sisters gazed interestedly at the spot where they had seen the last twirl of their mother's great round tail. Then Nassa came back and they followed her down under the root.

"The Little Prisoner"

from *Sajo and Her Beaver People* by Grey Owl

Chilawee and Chikanee are two beaver kittens, the pets of an Indian brother and sister, Shapian and Sajo. A trader takes Chikanee in payment for a debt, leaving Chilawee and the children heartbroken. The three set out on a long and dangerous journey to the city, hoping to find the little lost beaver.

And meanwhile what of Chikanee!

We must go back to the day the trader walked out of Gitchie Meegwon's camp with him, right out of the lives of his friends, it seemed, forever.

During the four or five days it took the trader, with his Ojibway canoe-men, to make the journey back to Rabbit Portage, Chikanee did not fare so badly, as one of the Indians took good care of him, keeping him well supplied with food and water. But he could not understand why Chilawee was not with him, and wondered where Sajo and Shapian had disappeared to. And he began to be lonesome for them all, and often cried out for Sajo to come to him, as she had always done when she heard the little beaver calling. But no one came except the stranger Indian, and then only to change his water and to give him food. This man, by the trader's orders, accompanied Chikanee on the steamboat to see that he arrived safely at the railroad, and there left him; the money for him was paid over to the Indian, and what happened to him now did not greatly matter.

Having now come to a stop, and thinking that he must be home again, he wailed loudly for liberty and recognition, expecting his playmates to come and take him out of this stuffy and uncomfortable box. But none came. So he started to chew at the box, and strange, harsh voices spoke angrily to him. He next tried to climb the walls of his prison, but they were too high, and these strangers shouted at him, and pounded on the box to keep him quiet, and now, thoroughly frightened, he lay still, whimpering and lonely. Where, oh where was Sajo, who had always comforted him in his small troubles, and in whose arms he had so often found such happiness? Where was Chilawee, from whom he had never before been separated for so much as an hour?

A little later he was loaded on to a train that thundered and roared its way for many hours. When the train first started, forgetting as he did to close his ears,* the noise drove him nearly crazy, and in his terror he tried to dive to freedom through his tiny dish of water, and upset it; so that besides his other misery he soon began to suffer from thirst. He had been snatched away from home too hurriedly for Sajo to have time to drop a bannock in the box, which would have lasted him several days, and no one now thought of providing him with anything to eat. And so, sick, hungry, lonesome, and wild with fear, he started desperately to cut his way out of the crate. In this he would have quickly succeeded, but striking a nail he broke one of his four cutting teeth, which made gnawing too painful to continue. His

*Beaver are able to open and close their ears, after the fashion of a purse, to keep out water and unpleasant sounds.

bedding, what little there was of it, became dirty, and the motion of the train thumped and bumped him against the hard sides of the box, so that he became bruised and sore. He tried hard to stay in the centre, away from the walls of his prison, but never could. One of the trainmen, intending to be kind, threw to him some crusts of bread from his own lunch, but he thought that the little beaver's frantic clutchings at his hands were a sign of ill-temper (he was just a wild animal to these people, who did not know that he only wanted to be helped), and from then on they were afraid of him—so small a little creature to be afraid of!—and no one attempted to give him any more bedding or food, and his water-dish remained empty for the same reason.

And he raised his voice in cries of misery and called and called for his small companions, who now could never hear him, wailed in his child-like voice for them to come and take away this great trouble that had befallen him. But no one paid any attention, if they ever even heard him, drowned as was his feeble outcry by the roar of the train.

At length, after many stops and starts, each of which jolted and slammed him from one hard side of his prison to the other, and a last, and cruelly rough ride in a delivery van, there came a sudden quietness. The cleats were taken from across the top of the box with a frightful screeching as the nails were drawn, and he was lifted out by a hand that held him very firmly by the tail; a large, strong hand, yet somehow a very gentle one. Then the other hand came up and was held against his chest as he hung head down, bringing him right end up, and a finger rubbed gently on one hot, tired little paw, and a deep voice spoke soothing words; so that suddenly he felt rather comfortable. For this man was a keeper of animals, and attendant in the Park where Chikanee was to stay, and he knew his business very well. And when he examined his small captive, and saw how miserable and bedraggled and covered with dirt the little creature was—he who had been so proud and careful of his coat!—the keeper said angrily to the delivery man (who, poor fellow, was not to blame at all):

"No water, nothing to eat, dry feet, dry tail, dry nose, teeth all broken up; if that isn't a shame, nothing ever was. Some way to ship a beaver, I'll say! But we'll soon fix you up, old-timer." For the man had been expecting his little guest, having had a letter about him, and had everything ready to receive him, and Chikanee soon found himself in an enclosure built of something like stone, but not nearly as friendly as stone, and surrounded by a rail of iron bars.

And in this gaol of iron and concrete Chikanee, for no crime at all, was to spend the rest of his days.

Chikanee, gentle, lovable Chikanee, was now supposed to be a wild and probably dangerous beast!

It was not a very large place, a mere hutch after the freedom of the big lake beside which he had spent most of his short life, but that did not matter for the moment—he smelled water! And then he saw, right in front of him, a deep, clear pool; not a very big one, to be sure, but at least it was water. Into this he immediately threw himself and drank thirstily, floating on the surface, while the cracked and dried-out tail and feet soaked up the, to him, life-giving moisture, and the cakes of dirt loosened and washed from off him as he swam slowly back and forth. This seemed like the beaver's heaven itself, after more than three days of noise, starvation, dirt, and utter misery, and the hot, fevered little body cooled off and all the bumps and bruises ceased to throb, as the cool water slowly got in its good work on him.

And now, he thought, this must be just the plunge-hole. Down there, somewhere, lay the entrance, and through this he would set out and would, no doubt, come to his home-lake, there to find his playmates on the shore; and then Chilawee would run to welcome him and roll on his woolly back with joy, and Sajo would come and pick him up, and hug him and make much of him, and whisper in his ear, and tickle him in that funny place

142

under his chin, and all these hard times would be forgotten.

So, with a great splurge he dived straight down—to strike his head on the hard bottom of the pool, almost stunning himself. Again he tried, with the same result. He scratched and bit at the concrete, thinking to tear his way through it to the tunnel that must, somewhere, lead out of it. But he only cracked and split his claws and took more chips out of his remaining teeth. Then he scrambled out of the pool and over to the bars, and tried to squeeze through them; but they were too close together. He tried to gnaw at them, but his broken teeth never even scratched them. So he ran round and round inside the enclosure, stopping here and there to dig, but to no purpose. For a long time he worked, running back to the pool and out again to the bars, trying to gnaw, trying to dig; but it was useless. And then at last he realized that there was no opening anywhere, no plunge-hole, no escape; and, weary, wretched and hopeless, he lay flat on the hard, hot floor of the pen and moaned, moaned as he had done when Sajo had nursed him to sleep whenever he had been lonesome—only then he had moaned with joy, and now it was from misery. And his little paws ached for just one touch of Chilawee's soft, silky fur. And now there was no Sajo, no Chilawee, only one unhappy Little Small in prison, all alone.

The attendant stood by for a long time, and watched and shook his head, and said "Too bad, little fellow, too bad." This was his job, taming these wild creatures that were sent to him from time to time; yet, liking animals as he did, he sometimes hated the work. To him they often seemed to be not wild things at all, but hopeless, unfortunate little people who could not speak, and who sometimes were so pitifully in need of the kindness for which they could not ask; and he had always felt that a man, who was so much bigger and stronger, and knew so many things that they did not, should be good to them and help them all he could. And he pitied the little beaver that was struggling so helplessly to be free, for this was not the first one that had come under his care,

144

and he knew their gentle nature. And stepping in through the gate of the pen, he picked up Chikanee carefully and cleverly, so that, as in the first place, he was not scared or excited, but was actually comfortable in his hands—they were so much more friendly than the concrete!

The keeper carried Chikanee to his cottage, which was close by, inside the Park. He had three young children, and when they saw their father bringing in a little beaver, they crowded round to see, and they shouted and clapped their hands with glee, so that Chikanee was afraid again, and tried to burrow into the man's coat; for already he had begun to trust him. And their father quieted the young ones and set the little creature on the floor, where, finding himself once more in a house, he felt a little more at home than in the cage. They all stood watching to see what he would do, and the keeper's wife said:

"The wee mite! Look how thin he is—Joey," to one of the youngsters, "go get an apple; those other beaver we used to have were just crazy for apples."

So this Joey fellow went and got one right away, and put it down on the floor in front of Chikanee. He had never seen an apple before, but he sniffed at it, and oh! what a wonderful smell came from it! And so he cut into it as best he could with his poor wee broken teeth and then, what a taste!—the most delicious taste in all the world! And seizing hold of this wonderful tit-bit with both hands, he demolished nearly the half of it. At this the keeper was very pleased, for some of his prisoners refused all food, and died, but now he knew that this one would recover; somehow he had been none too sure about it. And the delighted children laughed to see him sitting up there like a little man while he ate, and the keeper's wife exclaimed: "There, didn't I tell you? He'll be all right in no time."

Then the man brought in the sprays of fresh, juicy poplar leaves he had placed in the pen for him, but which he had not touched. But now he ate them, and the children wondered to see him holding the leaves in little bunches in his hands while he put them in his mouth. Feeling a good deal better by now, he made small sounds of pleasure while he ate, and at that the young ones marvelled even more, and one, a little girl with golden hair and a round, rosy face, said:

"Listen, listen to him talk, just like a little, wee baby. O daddy, do let's keep him in the kitchen!" And their mother spoke up too: "Yes, Alec, let's keep him here for a spell; there's no one in the Park—it's almost like putting a child in prison." And Alec answered:

"Perhaps you're right. We'll fix him a place in here for tonight."

So they made a place for our Chikanee in the kitchen, and Alec the keeper fastened a low, wide pan of water to the floor, and set a large box down on its side, with plenty of clean straw in it for a bed for him. And there the little beaver spent the night, not happily perhaps, but very comfortably.

The next morning Alec returned him to the pen, so that any of the public who came to the Park could see him; but when evening came round again and the grounds were empty, the keeper brought him back to the cottage. And from then on he did this every day, and Chikanee spent all the hours when he was not "working" in the keeper's house, and in the kitchen had his bed, and his big pan of water, and ate his leaves and twigs there. And each day he had a nice, juicy apple, which quite made up for a lot of his troubles, though not for all of them; for never would he be anything but lonesome, so long as he lived.* Every morning there was a considerable mess to clean up, of peeled sticks, and cut branches, and left-over leaves, and the floor was all slopped up with water, but the children willingly turned to and cleaned up, after he was carried away to his daily task of being stared at in the cage. Nobody seemed to mind the little trouble he was. He got

*Beaver possess probably the longest memory of any North American animal, much resembling the elephant in this respect.

146

along famously with the family and, in his own small way, soon became quite a part of the household.

As time went on he got to know them all, and he would romp clumsily with the youngsters; and to them he was a kind of tumbling, good-natured toy, a good deal like one of those roguish wool puppies to be found on Christmas trees. But to Chikanee, it could never be the same as it had been at O-pee-pee-soway, and often he didn't want to play, but lay quietly in his box, his little heart filled with a great empty longing for his old playmates.

Before very long his teeth had grown in, and he spent a lot of time sharpening them against one another, grinding and rattling them together at a great rate.† His coat, which he had sadly neglected for a time, so that it had become all tangled and awry, now got its daily scrubbing and combing, and his small frame, that had for a while been little more than a bag of bones, soon filled out, and he began to look like the old Chikanee again. And in a way he was happy; but never quite.

While in the cage he was really miserable, and the keeper knew this, and always felt badly when he put the little fellow in there each morning, and looked back at this pitiful little creature that gazed after him so wistfully as he walked away, sitting there alone on the bare cement floor, surrounded by bars that would have held a grizzly bear. He remembered that a beaver may live more than twenty years—twenty years in that prison of iron and concrete! In twenty years his own family would be grown up and away from there; he himself might be gone. The town would have become a great city (it was not really a very big place); people would come and go—free people, happy people—and through it all, this unhappy little beast, who had done no harm to anyone, and seemed only to want someone to be kind to him, would, for twenty long and lonely years, look out through the bars of that wretched pen as though he had been some violent

†A beaver's teeth grow continuously, and they grind and sharpen them constantly, as do porcupines, muskrats, and some other rodents.

147

criminal; waiting for the freedom that would never be his, waiting only to die at last. And, thought the keeper, for no good reason at all, except that a few thoughtless people, who never really cared if they ever saw a beaver, might stare for a minute or two at the disconsolate little prisoner, and then go away and forget they had ever seen him. Somehow it did not seem fair, to this kind-hearted man, and when he watched the little creature rollicking with the children in his funny, clumsy way, he wished very much that there was something that he could do about it, and decided to make his small prisoner as happy as he could, and give him the freedom of the cottage as long as it was at all possible.

But Chikanee had not quite given up; he had one hope that for a long time he never lost. He quite expected that, in some mysterious way, Chilawee would come to join him; for in the old days, no matter where he had happened to be, it had not been long before Chilawee had turned up, looking for him. And so, every so often, he searched for him very carefully, looking in the wooden hut that stood in the enclosure, going patiently all though the downstairs rooms of the cottage, and would sometimes take a run outside and examine the woodshed very thoroughly, and was very sure that some day he would find him. But after a whole month of daily disappointments he began to lose courage, and at last gave up his search that always turned out to be such a failure.

And hundreds of miles away, Chilawee was doing the very same thing, and all for nothing.

Chikanee was just commencing to get over this when something took place that was the very worst of all—and yet something that was very near to his dearest wish. One day an Indian woman, with a bright shawl on her head, passed by the pen. The moment he saw her, Chikanee dashed wildly at the bars, and reached through them with clutching paws, and let out a piercing cry, for fear she would pass him by; at which the woman stopped and spoke to him, and the sounds she made

were the same as he had heard so often in the Indian country, at home! But not the voice. And seeing her face, and catching the scent of her, he turned and plodded slowly back to the bare wooden hut again, more dejected and downcast than he had ever been.

He had thought it was Sajo.

But this experience stirred him, and brought new hopes to him; he got the idea that some day Sajo *would* come. And from then on he watched for her. Crowds of people visited the Park in the afternoons, and most of them paused by his cage to see what a beaver was like. But his "customers" never stayed long, and soon passed on; to most of them he looked to be just a scrubby little pup with a flat tail. Some just gazed carelessly, others curiously; a few poked sticks at him and made harsh and, as he thought, threatening sounds; a few, a very few pitied him, and one or two were friendly and gave him peanuts and candy—but none of them was Sajo. But he continued to hope, and spent his time watching closely every face he saw, sniffing every hand he could get near to. But he never saw the face he looked for, never caught the scent of that so-loved little hand. Yet he was sure that some day a well-remembered voice would call out "Chik-a-*nee!*", that the small brown hands whose touch had so often thrilled his little body, would again pick him up, and then—Oh! the joy of once more pushing his nose close into that special spot in a certain warm, soft neck, there to puff and blow a little while and then to slumber, and forget!

Hours at a time he spent this way, watching, waiting, hoping; and later, on his little pallet in the kitchen, he would think, in some dim and misty way, of the happy days that seemed now to have been oh, so long ago, and thought of the little chamber under Shapian's bed, that Chilawee and he had between them for their very own, and of the crazy, tiny beaver house, and all the other arrangements at which they had worked so bravely together. And at last he became listless, and kept to himself, even

150

when he was supposed to be happy in the kitchen; and he never played with the children any more. He neglected his coat, so that it became matted and unkempt. And he began to refuse his food, and would sit with his apple untouched in his hands, his little head drooping, eyes closed, breathing fast and heavily.

And the keeper, looking at him sorrowfully, knew that there was no longer any need to worry about the twenty years; or any years.

Chikanee wasn't going to live.

And the wee brain grew hot and feverish with longing, and he seemed sometimes almost to see his old play-fellows there before him, and thinking of them fell asleep, and sleeping dreamed of them. For animals *do* dream, as perhaps you know, and often wake up half scared to pieces from a nightmare, the same as you or I, and from the sounds they sometimes make, some of their dreams must be quite pleasant, too.

One evening he awoke from a dream of them that was so real that he thought himself once more at home with them, and he got up and ran whimpering about the kitchen, looking for them, and not finding them, cried out again and again in loud sobbing wails, from very lonesomeness and misery.

And as he cried, his voice was like the voice of a small, lost child.

For he did not, could not know, that less than one mile away, in another and similar room, was another and similar little beaver, and that there with him, waiting for morning, too excited to even think of sleeping, were two little Indians—a boy that stood straight and proudly, like an arrow, and a little girl who had on a brightly coloured head-shawl.

And in one corner of the room there stood an old familiar, well-worn, birch-bark basket.

Yes, you guessed it. Sajo and Shapian had really come, at last.

"Vanity and Vexation of Spirit"

from *Anne of Green Gables*
by L. M. Montgomery

Marilla, walking home one late April evening from an Aid meeting, realized that the winter was over and gone with the thrill and delight that spring never fails to bring to the oldest and saddest as well as to the youngest and merriest. Marilla was not given to subjective analysis of her thoughts and feelings. She probably imagined that she was thinking about the Aids and their missionary box and the new carpet for the vestry-room, but under these reflections was a harmonious consciousness of red fields smoking into pale-purply mists in the declining sun, of long, sharp-pointed fir shadows falling over the meadow beyond the brook, of still, crimson-budded maples around a mirror-like wood-pool, of a wakening in the world and a stir of hidden pulses under the grey sod. The spring was abroad in the land and Marilla's sober, middle-aged step was lighter and swifter because of its deep, primal gladness.

Her eyes dwelt affectionately on Green Gables, peering through its network of trees and reflecting the sunlight back from its windows in several little coruscations of glory. Marilla, as she picked her steps along the damp lane, thought that it was really a satisfaction to know that she was going home to a briskly snapping wood fire and a table nicely spread for tea, instead of to the cold comfort of old Aid meeting evenings before Anne had come to Green Gables.

Consequently, when Marilla entered her kitchen and found the fire black out, with no sign of Anne anywhere, she felt justly disappointed and irritated. She had told Anne to be sure and have tea ready at five o'clock, but now she must hurry to take off her second-best dress and prepare the meal herself against Matthew's return from ploughing.

"I'll settle Miss Anne when she comes home," said Marilla grimly, as she shaved up kindlings with a carving knife and more vim than was strictly necessary. Matthew had come in and was waiting patiently for his tea in his corner. "She's gadding off somewhere with Diana, writing stories or practising dialogues or some such tomfoolery, and never thinking once about the time or her duties. She's just got to be pulled up short and sudden on this sort of thing. I don't care if Mrs. Allan does say she's the brightest and sweetest child she ever knew. She may be bright and sweet enough, but her head is full of nonsense and there's never any knowing what shape it'll break out in next. Just as soon as she grows out of one freak she takes up with another. But there! Here I am saying the very thing I was riled with Rachel Lynde for saying at the Aid today. I was real glad when Mrs. Allan spoke up for Anne, for if she hadn't I know I'd have said something too sharp to Rachel before everybody. Anne's got plenty of faults, goodness knows, and far be it from me to deny it. But I'm bringing her up and not Rachel Lynde, who'd pick faults in the Angel Gabriel himself if he lived in Avonlea. Just the same, Anne has no business to leave the house like this when I told her she was to stay home this afternoon and look after things. I must say, with all her faults, I never found her disobedient or untrustworthy before and I'm real sorry to find her so now."

"Well now, I dunno," said Matthew, who, being patient and wise and, above all, hungry, had deemed it best to let Marilla talk her wrath out unhindered, having learned by experience that she got through with whatever work was on hand much quicker if not delayed by untimely argument. "Perhaps you're judging her too hasty, Marilla. Don't call her untrustworthy until you're sure she has disobeyed you. Mebbe it can all be explained—Anne's a great hand at explaining."

"She's not here when I told her to stay," retorted Marilla. "I reckon she'll find it hard to explain *that* to my satisfaction. Of course I knew you'd take her part, Matthew. But I'm bringing her up, not you."

It was dark when supper was ready, and still no sign of Anne, coming hurriedly over the log bridge or up Lovers' Lane, breathless and repentant with a sense of neglected duties. Marilla washed and put away the dishes grimly. Then, wanting a candle to light her down cellar, she went up to the east gable for the one that generally stood on Anne's table. Lighting it, she turned around to see Anne herself lying on the bed, face downward among the pillows.

"Mercy on us," said astonished Marilla, "have you been asleep, Anne?"

"No," was the muffled reply.

"Are you sick then?" demanded Marilla anxiously, going over to the bed.

Anne cowered deeper into her pillows as if desirous of hiding herself forever from mortal eyes.

"No. But please, Marilla, go away and don't look at me. I'm in the depths of despair and I don't care who gets head in class or writes the best composition or sings in the Sunday school choir any more. Little things like that are of no importance now because I don't suppose I'll ever be able to go anywhere again. My career is closed. Please, Marilla, go away and don't look at me."

"Did anyone ever hear the like?" the mystified Marilla wanted to know. "Anne Shirley, whatever is the matter with you? What have you done? Get right up this minute and tell me. This minute, I say. There now, what is it?"

Anne had slid to the floor in despairing obedience.

"Look at my hair, Marilla," she whispered.

Accordingly, Marilla lifted her candle and looked scrutinizingly at Anne's hair, flowing in heavy masses down her back. It certainly had a very strange appearance.

"Anne Shirley, what have you done to your hair? Why, it's *green!*"

Green it might be called, if it were any earthly colour— a queer, dull, bronzy green, with streaks here and there of the original red to heighten the ghastly effect. Never in all her life had Marilla seen anything so grotesque as Anne's hair at that moment.

"Yes, it's green," moaned Anne. "I thought nothing could be as bad as red hair. But now I know it's ten times worse to have green hair. Oh, Marilla, you little know how utterly wretched I am."

"I little know how you got into this fix, but I mean to find out," said Marilla. "Come right down to the kitchen—it's too cold up here—and tell me just what you've done. I've been expecting something queer for some time. You haven't got into any scrape for over two months, and I was sure another one was due. Now, then, what did you do to your hair?"

"I dyed it."

"Dyed it! Dyed your hair! Anne Shirley, didn't you know it was a wicked thing to do?"

"Yes, I knew it was a little wicked," admitted Anne. "But I thought it was worthwhile to be a little wicked to get rid of red hair. I counted the cost, Marilla. Besides, I meant to be extra good in other ways to make up for it."

"Well," said Marilla sarcastically, "if I'd decided it was worthwhile to dye my hair I'd have dyed it a decent colour at least. I wouldn't have dyed it green.''

''But I didn't mean to dye it green, Marilla,'' protested Anne dejectedly. ''If I was wicked I meant to be wicked to some purpose. He said it would turn my hair a beautiful raven black—he positively assured me that it would. How could I doubt his word, Marilla? I know what it feels like to have your word doubted. And Mrs. Allan says we should never suspect anyone of not telling us the truth unless we have proof that they're not. I have proof now—green hair is proof enough for anybody. But I hadn't then and I believed every word he said *implicitly*.''

''Who said? Who are you talking about?''

"The pedlar that was here this afternoon. I bought the dye from him."

"Anne Shirley, how often have I told you never to let one of those pedlars in the house! I don't believe in encouraging them to come around at all."

"Oh, I didn't let him in the house. I remembered what you told me, and I went out, carefully shut the door, and looked at his things on the step. He had a big box full of very interesting things and he told me he was working hard to make enough money to bring his wife and children out from Germany. He spoke so feelingly about them that it touched my heart. I wanted to buy

something from him to help him in such a worthy project. Then all at once I saw the bottle of hair dye. The pedlar said it was warranted to dye any hair to a beautiful raven black and wouldn't wash off. In a trice I saw myself with beautiful raven black hair and the temptation was irresistible. But the price of the bottle was seventy-five cents and I had only fifty cents left out of my chicken money. I think the pedlar had a very kind heart, for he said that, seeing it was me, he'd sell it for fifty cents and that was just giving it away. So I bought it, and as soon as he had gone I came up here and applied it with an old hair-brush as the directions said. I used up the whole bottle, and oh, Marilla, when I saw the dreadful colour it turned my hair I repented of being wicked, I can tell you. And I've been repenting ever since."

"Well, I hope you'll repent to good purpose," said Marilla severely, "and that you've got your eyes opened to where your vanity has led you, Anne. Goodness knows what's to be done. I suppose the first thing is to give your hair a good washing and see if that will do any good."

Accordingly, Anne washed her hair, scrubbing it vigorously with soap and water, but for all the difference it made she might as well have been scouring its original red. The pedlar had certainly spoken the truth when he declared that the dye wouldn't wash off, however his veracity might be impeached in other respects.

"Oh, Marilla, what shall I do?" questioned Anne in tears. "I can never live this down. People have pretty well forgotten my other mistakes —the liniment cake and setting Diana drunk and flying into a temper with Mrs. Lynde. But they'll never forget this. They will think I am not respectable. Oh, Marilla, 'what a tangled web we weave when first we practise to deceive.' That is poetry, but it is true. And oh, how Josie Pye will laugh! Marilla, I *cannot* face Josie Pye. I am the unhappiest girl in Prince Edward Island."

Anne's unhappiness continued for a week. During that time

she went nowhere and shampooed her hair every day. Diana alone of outsiders knew the fatal secret, but she promised solemnly never to tell, and it may be stated here and now that she kept her word. At the end of the week Marilla said decidedly:

"It's no use, Anne. That is fast dye if ever there was any. Your hair must be cut off; there is no other way. You can't go out with it looking like that."

Anne's lips quivered, but she realized the bitter truth of Marilla's remarks. With a dismal sigh she went for the scissors.

"Please cut it off at once, Marilla, and have it over. Oh, I feel that my heart is broken. This is such an unromantic affliction. The girls in books lose their hair in fevers or sell it to get money for some good deed, and I'm sure I wouldn't mind losing my hair in some such fashion half so much. But there is nothing comforting in having your hair cut off because you've dyed it a dreadful colour, is there? I'm going to weep all the time you're cutting it off, if it won't interfere. It seems such a tragic thing."

Anne wept then, but later on, when she went upstairs and looked at the glass, she was calm with despair. Marilla had done her work thoroughly and it had been necessary to shingle the hair as closely as possible. The result was not becoming, to state the case as mildly as may be. Anne promptly turned her glass to the wall.

"I'll never, never look at myself again until my hair grows," she exclaimed passionately.

Then she suddenly righted the glass.

"Yes, I will, too. I'd do penance for being wicked that way. I'll look at myself every time I come to my room and see how ugly I am. And I won't try to imagine it away, either. I never thought I was vain about my hair, of all things, but now I know I was, in spite of its being red, because it was so long and thick and curly. I expect something will happen to my nose next."

Anne's clipped head made a sensation in school on the following Monday, but to her relief nobody guessed the real

161

reason for it, not even Josie Pye, who, however, did not fail to inform Anne that she looked like a perfect scarecrow.

"I didn't say anything when Josie said that to me," Anne confided that evening to Marilla, who was lying on the sofa after one of her headaches, "because I thought it was part of my punishment and I ought to bear it patiently. It's hard to be told you look like a scarecrow and I wanted to say something back. But I didn't. I just swept her one scornful look and then I forgave her. It makes you feel very virtuous when you forgive people, doesn't it? I mean to devote all my energies to being good after this and I shall never try to be beautiful again. Of course it's better to be good. I know it is, but it's sometimes so hard to believe a thing even when you know it. I do really want to be good, Marilla, like you and Mrs. Allan and Miss Stacy, and grow up to be a credit to you. Diana says when my hair begins to grow to tie a black velvet ribbon around my head with a bow at one side. She says she thinks it will be very becoming. I will call it a snood—that sounds so romantic. But am I talking too much, Marilla? Does it hurt your head?"

"My head is better now. It was terrible bad this afternoon, though. These headaches of mine are getting worse and worse. I'll have to see a doctor about them. As for your chatter, I don't know that I mind it—I've got so used to it."

Which was Marilla's way of saying that she liked to hear it.

Silverspot

by Ernest Thompson Seton

How many of us have ever got to know a wild animal? I do not mean merely to meet with one once or twice, or to have one in a cage, but to really know it for a long time while it is wild, and to get an insight into its life and history. The trouble usually is to know one creature from his fellow. One fox or crow is so much like another that we cannot be sure that it really is the same next time we meet. But once in awhile there rises an animal who is stronger or wiser than his fellow, who becomes a great leader, who is, as we would say, a genius, and if he is bigger, or has some mark by which men can know him, he soon becomes famous in his country, and shows us that the life of a wild animal may be far more interesting and exciting than that of many human beings.

Of this class were Courtrand, the bob-tailed wolf that terrorized the whole city of Paris for about ten years in the beginning of the fourteenth century; Clubfoot, the lame grizzly bear that left such a terrific record in the San Joaquin Valley of California; Lobo, the king-wolf of New Mexico, that killed a cow every day for five years, and the Soehnee panther that in less than two years killed nearly three hundred human beings—and such also was Silverspot, whose history, so far as I could learn it, I shall now briefly tell.

Silverspot was simply a wise old crow; his name was given because of the silvery white spot that was like a nickel, stuck on his right side, between the eye and the bill, and it was owing to this spot that I was able to know him from the other crows, and put together the parts of his history that came to my knowledge.

Crows are, as you must know, our most intelligent birds—'Wise as an old crow' did not become a saying without good reason. Crows know the value of organization, and are as well drilled as soldiers—very much better than some soldiers, in fact, for crows are always on duty, always at war, and always dependent on each other for life and safety. Their leaders not only are the oldest and wisest of the band, but also the strongest and bravest, for they must be ready at any time with sheer force to put down an upstart or a rebel. The rank and file are the youngsters and the crows without special gifts.

Old Silverspot was the leader of a large band of crows that made their headquarters near Toronto, Canada, in Castle Frank, which is a pine-clad hill on the northeast edge of the city. This band numbered about two hundred, and for reasons that I never understood did not increase. In mild winters they stayed along the Niagara River; in cold winters they went much farther south. But each year in the last week of February Old Silverspot would muster his followers and boldly cross the forty miles of open water that lies between Toronto and Niagara; not, however, in a straight line would he go, but always in a curve to the west, whereby he kept in sight of the familiar landmark of Dundas Mountain, until the pine-clad hill itself came in view. Each year he came with his troop, and for about six weeks took up his abode on the hill. Each morning thereafter the crows set out in three bands to forage. One band went southeast to Ashbridge's Bay. One went north up the Don, and one, the largest, went northwestward up the ravine. The last Silverspot led in person. Who led the others I never found out.

On calm mornings they flew high and straight away. But when

it was windy the band flew low, and followed the ravine for shelter. My windows overlooked the ravine, and it was thus that in 1885 I first noticed this old crow. I was a new-comer in the neighbourhood, but an old resident said to me then "that there old crow has been a-flying up and down this ravine for more than twenty years." My chances to watch were in the ravine, and Silverspot doggedly clinging to the old route, though now it was edged with houses and spanned by bridges, became a very familiar acquaintance. Twice each day in March and part of April, then again in the late summer and the fall, he passed and repassed, and gave me chances to see his movements, and hear his orders to his bands, and so, little by little, opened my eyes to the fact that the crows, though a little people, are of great wit, a race of birds with a language and a social system that is wonderfully human in many of its chief points, and in some is better carried out than our own.

One windy day I stood on the high bridge across the ravine, as the old crow, heading his long, straggling troop, came flying down homeward. Half a mile away I could hear the contented *'All's well, come right along!'* as we should say, or as he put it, and as also

No. 1.

Caw   **Caw**

his lieutenant echoed it at the rear of the band. They were flying very low to be out of the wind, and would have to rise a little to clear the bridge on which I was. Silverspot saw me standing there, and as I was closely watching him he didn't like it. He checked his flight and called out, *'Be on your guard,'* or

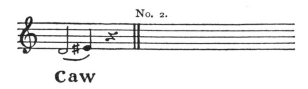

Caw

and rose much higher in the air. Then seeing that I was not armed he flew over my head about twenty feet, and his followers in turn did the same, dipping again to the old level when past the bridge.

Next day I was at the same place, and as the crows came near I raised my walking stick and pointed it at them. The old fellow at once cried out *'Danger,'* and rose fifty feet higher than before.

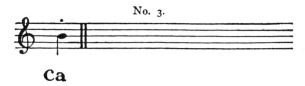

Ca

Seeing that it was not a gun, he ventured to fly over. But on the third day I took with me a gun, and at once he cried out, *'Great danger—a gun.'* His lieutenant repeated the cry,

ca ca ca ca Caw

and every crow in the troop began to tower and scatter from the rest, till they were far above gun shot, and so passed safely over, coming down again to the shelter of the valley when well beyond reach. Another time, as the long, straggling troop came down the valley, a red-tailed hawk alighted on a tree close by their intended route. The leader cried out, *'Hawk, hawk,'* and stayed his flight, as

No. 5.

Caw   Caw

did each crow on nearing him, until all were massed in a solid
body. Then, no longer fearing the hawk, they passed on. But a
quarter of a mile farther on a man with a gun appeared below,
and the cry, *'Great danger—a gun, a gun; scatter for your lives,'* at

No. 6.

ca ca ca ca Caw

once caused them to scatter widely and tower till far beyond
range. Many others of his words of command I learned in the
course of my long acquaintance, and found that sometimes a very
little difference in the sound makes a very great difference in
meaning. Thus while No. 5 means hawk, or any large, dangerous
bird, this means *'wheel around,'* evidently a combination of No. 5,
whose root idea is danger, and of No. 4, whose root idea is
retreat,

No. 7.

Caw   Caw   ca ca ca ca

and this again is a mere *'good day,'* to a far away comrade.

No. 8.

Caw   Caw

167

This is usually addressed to the ranks and means *'attention'*.

No. 9.

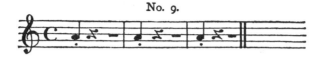

Early in April there began to be great doings among the crows. Some new cause of excitement seemed to have come on them. They spent half the day among the pines, instead of foraging from dawn till dark. Pairs and trios might be seen chasing each other, and from time to time they showed off in various feats of flight. A favourite sport was to dart down suddenly from a great height toward some perching crow, and just before touching it to turn at a hairbreadth and rebound in the air so fast that the wings of the swooper whirred with a sound like distant thunder. Sometimes one crow would lower his head, raise every feather, and coming close to another would gurgle out a long note like

No. 10.

C – r – r – r – a – w

What did it all mean? I soon learned. They were making love and pairing off. The males were showing off their wing powers and their voices to the lady crows. And they must have been highly appreciated, for by the middle of April all had mated and had scattered over the country for their honeymoon, leaving the sombre old pines of Castle Frank deserted and silent.

The Sugar Loaf hill stands alone in the Don Valley. It is still covered with woods that join with those of Castle Frank, a quarter of a mile off. In the woods, between the two hills, is a pine-tree in whose top is a deserted hawk's nest. Every Toronto school-boy knows the nest, and, excepting that I had once shot a

168

black squirrel on its edge, no one had ever seen a sign of life about it. There it was year after year, ragged and old, and falling to pieces. Yet, strange to tell, in all that time it never did drop to pieces, like other old nests.

One morning in May I was out at grey dawn, and stealing gently through the woods, whose dead leaves were so wet that no rustle was made. I chanced to pass under the old nest, and was surprised to see a black tail sticking over the edge. I struck the tree a smart blow, off flew a crow, and the secret was out. I had long suspected that a pair of crows nested each year about the pines, but now I realized that it was Silverspot and his wife. The old nest was theirs, and they were too wise to give it an air of spring-cleaning and housekeeping each year. Here they had nested for long, though guns in the hands of men and boys hungry to shoot crows were carried under their home every day. I never surprised the old fellow again, though I several times saw him through my telescope.

One day while watching I saw a crow crossing the Don Valley with something white in his beak. He flew to the mouth of the Rosedale Brook, then took a short flight to the Beaver Elm. There he dropped the white object, and looking about gave me a chance to recognize my old friend Silverspot. After a minute he picked up the white thing—a shell—and walked over past the spring, and here, among the docks and the skunk-cabbages, he unearthed a pile of shells and other white, shiny things. He spread them out in the sun, turned them over, lifted them one by one in his beak, dropped them, nestled on them as though they were eggs, toyed with them and gloated over them like a miser. This was his hobby, his weakness. He could not have explained *why* he enjoyed them, any more than a boy can explain why he collects postage-stamps, or a girl why she prefers pearls to rubies; but his pleasure in them was very real, and after half an hour he covered them all, including the new one, with earth and leaves, and flew off. I went at once to the spot and examined the hoard;

169

there was about a hatful in all, chiefly white pebbles, clam-shells, and some bits of tin, but there was also the handle of a china cup, which must have been the gem of the collection. That was the last time I saw them. Silverspot knew that I had found his treasures, and he removed them at once; where I never knew.

During the space that I watched him so closely he had many little adventures and escapes. He was once severely handled by a sparrowhawk, and often he was chased and worried by kingbirds. Not that these did him much harm, but they were such noisy pests that he avoided their company as quickly as possible, just as a grown man avoids a conflict with a noisy and impudent small boy. He had some cruel tricks, too. He had a way of going the round of the small birds' nests each morning to eat the new laid eggs, as regularly as a doctor visiting his patients. But we must not judge him for that, as it is just what we ourselves do to the hens in the barnyard.

His quickness of wit was often shown. One day I saw him flying down the ravine with a large piece of bread in his bill. The stream below him was at this time being bricked over as a sewer. There was one part of two hundred yards quite finished, and, as he flew over the open water just above this, the bread fell from his bill, and was swept by the current out of sight into the tunnel. He flew down and peered vainly into the dark cavern, then, acting upon a happy thought, he flew to the downstream end of the tunnel, and awaiting the reappearance of the floating bread, as it was swept onward by the current, he seized and bore it off in triumph.

Silverspot was a crow of the world. He was truly a successful crow. He lived in a region that, though full of dangers, abounded with food. In the old, unrepaired nest he raised a brood each year with his wife, whom, by the way, I never could distinguish, and when the crows again gathered together he was their acknowledged chief.

The reassembling takes place about the end of June—the young crows with their bob-tails, soft wings, and falsetto voices are brought by their parents, whom they nearly equal in size, and introduced to society at the old pine woods, a woods that is at once their fortress and college. Here they find security in numbers and in lofty yet sheltered perches, and here they begin their schooling and are taught all the secrets of success in crow life, and in crow life the least failure does not simply mean begin again. It means *death*.

The first week or two after their arrival is spent by the young ones in getting acquainted, for each crow must know personally all the others in the band. Their parents meanwhile have time to rest a little after the work of raising them; for now the youngsters are able to feed themselves and roost on a branch in a row, just like big folks.

In a week or two the moulting season comes. At this time the old crows are usually irritable and nervous, but it does not stop them from beginning to drill the youngsters, who, of course, do not much enjoy the punishment and nagging they get so soon after they have been mamma's own darlings. But it is all for their good, as the old lady said when she skinned the eels, and old Silverspot is an excellent teacher. Sometimes he seems to make a speech to them. What he says I cannot guess, but, judging by the way they receive it, it must be extremely witty. Each morning there is a company drill, for the young ones naturally drop into two or three squads according to their age and strength. The rest of the day they forage with their parents.

When at length September comes we find a great change. The rabble of silly little crows have begun to learn sense. The delicate blue iris of their eyes, the sign of a fool-crow, has given place to the dark brown eye of the old stager. They know their drill now and have learned sentry duty. They have been taught guns and traps and taken a special course in wireworms and greencorn. They know that a fat old farmer's wife is much less dangerous, though so much larger, than her fifteen-year-old son, and they can tell the boy from his sister. They know that an umbrella is not a gun, and they can count up to six, which is fair for young crows, though Silverspot can go up nearly to thirty. They know the smell of gun-powder and the south side of a hemlock-tree, and begin to plume themselves upon being crows of the world. They always fold their wings three times after alighting, to be sure that it is neatly done. They know how to worry a fox into giving up half his dinner, and also that when the kingbird or the purple martin assails them they must dash into a bush, for it is as impossible to fight the little pests as it is for the fat apple-woman to catch the small boys who have raided her basket. All these things do the young crows know; but they have taken no lessons in egg-hunting yet, for it is not the season. They are unacquainted with clams, and have never tasted horses' eyes, or seen sprouted corn, and they don't know a thing about travel, the greatest educator of all. They did not think of that two months ago, and since then they have thought of it, but have learned to wait till their betters are ready.

September sees a great change in the old crows, too. Their moulting is over. They are now in full feather again and proud of their handsome coats. Their health is again good, and with it their tempers are improved. Even old Silverspot, the strict teacher, becomes quite jolly, and the youngsters, who have long ago learned to respect him, begin really to love him.

He has hammered away at drill, teaching them all the signals and words of command in use, and now it is a pleasure to see them in the early morning.

'Company One!' the old chieftain would cry in crow, and Company One would answer with a great clamour.

'Fly!' and himself leading them, they would all fly straight forward.

'Mount!' and straight upward they turned in a moment.

'Bunch!' and they all massed into a dense black flock.

'Scatter!' and they spread out like leaves before the wind.

'*Form line!*' and they strung out into the long line of ordinary flight.

'*Descend!*' and they all dropped nearly to the ground.

'*Forage!*' and they alighted and scattered about to feed, while two of the permanent sentries mounted duty—one on a tree to the right, the other on a mound to the far left. A minute or two later Silverspot would cry out, '*A man with a gun!*' The sentries repeated the cry and the company flew at once in open order as quickly as possible toward the trees. Once behind these, they formed line again in safety and returned to the home pines.

Sentry duty is not taken in turn by all the crows, but a certain number whose watchfulness has been often proved are the perpetual sentries, and are expected to watch and forage at the same time. Rather hard on them it seems to us, but it works well and the crow organization is admitted by all birds to be the very best in existence.

Finally, each November sees the troop sail away southward to learn new modes of life, new landmarks and new kinds of food, under the guidance of the ever-wise Silverspot.

There is only one time when a crow is a fool, and that is at night. There is only one bird that terrifies the crow, and that is the owl. When, therefore, these come together it is a woeful thing for the sable birds. The distant hoot of an owl after dark is enough to make them withdraw their heads from under their wings, and sit trembling and miserable till morning. In very cold weather the exposure of their faces thus has often resulted in a crow having one or both of his eyes frozen, so that blindness followed and therefore death. There are no hospitals for sick crows.

But with the morning their courage comes again, and arousing themselves they ransack the woods for a mile around till they find that owl, and if they do not kill him they at least worry him half to death and drive him twenty miles away.

In 1893 the crows had come as usual to Castle Frank. I was

walking in these woods a few days afterward when I chanced upon the track of a rabbit that had been running at full speed over the snow and dodging about among the trees as though pursued. Strange to tell, I could see no track of the pursuer. I followed the trail and presently saw a drop of blood on the snow, and a little farther on found the partly devoured remains of a little brown bunny. What had killed him was a mystery until a careful search showed in the snow a great double-toed track and a beautifully pencilled brown feather. Then all was clear—*a horned owl.* Half an hour later, in passing again by the place, there, in a tree, within ten feet of the bones of his victim, was the fierce-eyed owl himself. The murderer still hung about the scene of his crime. For once circumstantial evidence had not lied. At my approach he gave a guttural *'grrr-oo'* and flew off with low flagging flight to haunt the distant sombre woods.

Two days afterward, at dawn, there was a great uproar among the crows. I went out early to see, and found some black feathers drifting over the snow. I followed up the wind in the direction from which they came and soon saw the bloody remains of a crow and the great double-toed track which again told me that the murderer was the owl. All around were signs of the struggle, but the fell destroyer was too strong. The poor crow had been dragged from his perch at night, when the darkness had put him at a hopeless disadvantage.

I turned over the remains, and by chance unburied the head—then started with an exclamation of sorrow. Alas! It was the head of old Silverspot. His long life of usefulness to his tribe was over—slain at last by the owl that he had taught so many hundreds of young crows to beware of.

The old nest on the Sugar Loaf is abandoned now. The crows still come in spring-time to Castle Frank, but without their famous leader their numbers are dwindling, and soon they will be seen no more about the old pine-grove in which they and their forefathers had lived and learned for ages.

"Doctor and Dentist"

from *The Book of Small* by Emily Carr

Emily Carr was a great Canadian artist, as well as a skilful, sensitive writer, and a fascinating personality. In The Book of Small, *from which this selection is taken, she tells what it was like to grow up in Victoria, British Columbia, in the last two decades of the nineteenth century.*

When Victoria was young, specialists had not been invented—the Family Doctor did you all over. You did not have a special doctor for each part. Dr. Helmcken attended to all our ailments—Father's gout, our stomach-aches; he even told us what to do once when the cat had fits. If he was wanted in a hurry he got there in no time and did not wait for you to become sicker so that he could make a bigger cure. You began to get better the moment you heard Dr. Helmcken coming up the stairs. He did have the most horrible medicines—castor oil, Gregory's powder, blue pills, black draughts, sulphur and treacle.

Jokey people called him Dr. Heal-my-skin. He had been Doctor in the old Fort and knew everybody in Victoria. He was very thin, very active, very cheery. He had an old brown mare called Julia. When the Doctor came to see Mother we fed Julia at the gate with clover. The Doctor loved old Julia. One stormy night he was sent for because Mother was very ill. He came very quickly and Mother said, "I am sorry to bring you and Julia out on such a night, Doctor."

"Julia is in her stable. What was the good of two of us getting wet?" he replied.

My little brother fell across a picket fence once and tore his leg. The Doctor put him on our dining-room sofa and sewed it up. The servant came rushing in to say, "House all burn up!" Dr. Helmcken put in the last stitch, wiped his needle on his coat sleeve and put it into his case, then, stripping off his coat, rushed to the kitchen pump and pumped till the fire was put out.

Once I knelt on a needle which broke into my knee. While I was telling Mother about it who should come up the steps but the Doctor! He had just looked in to see the baby who had not been very well. They put me on the kitchen table. The Doctor cut slits in my knee and wiggled his fingers round inside it for three hours hunting for the pieces of needle. They did not know the way of drawing bits out with a magnet then, nor did they give chloroform for little things like that.

The Doctor said, "Yell, lassie, yell! It will let the pain out." I did yell, but the pain stayed in.

I remember the Doctor's glad voice as he said, "Thank God, I have got all of it now, or the lassie would have been lame for life with that under her knee cap!" Then he washed his hands under the kitchen tap and gave me a peppermint.

Dr. Helmcken knew each part of every one of us. He could have taken us to pieces and put us together again without mixing up any of our legs or noses or anything.

Dr. Helmcken's office was a tiny two-room cottage on the lower end of Fort Street near Wharf Street. It sat in a hummocky field; you walked along two planks and came to three steps and the door. The outer room had a big table in the centre filled with

bottles of all sizes and shapes. All were empty and all dusty.
Round the walls of the room were shelves with more bottles, all
full, and lots of musty old books. The inner office had a stove and
was very higgledy-piggledy. He would allow no one to go in and
tidy it up.

The Doctor sat in a round-backed wooden chair before a table;
there were three kitchen chairs against the wall for invalids. He
took you over to a very dirty, uncurtained window, jerked up the
blind and said, "Tongue!" Then he poked you round the middle
so hard that things fell out of your pockets. He put a wooden
trumpet band down on your chest and stuck his ear to the other
end. After listening and grunting he went into the bottle room,
took a bottle, blew the dust off it and emptied out the dead flies.

Then he went to the shelves and filled it from several other bottles, corked it, gave it to Mother and sent you home to get well on it. He stood on the step and lit a new cigar after every patient as if he was burning up your symptoms to make room for the next sick person.

Victoria's dentist was a different sort of person. He shammed. "Toothache, eh?" he said in a "pretend" sorry voice with his nose twisted against one cheek or the other as if he felt the pain most awfully himself. He sat you in a green plush chair and wound you up to his eye. Then he took your head in his wide red hand that smelled of fancy soap and pushed back your cheek, saying, "Let me just see—I am not going to do anything." All the time he was taking something from a tray behind you and, before you knew where you were, he had nearly pulled the head off your neck.

I shouted, "You lied!" and got slapped as well as extracted, while the blood ran down my chin.

My Father never had a toothache till he was sixty years of age, nor did he lose a tooth. When the dentist said four of my second teeth needed to be filled, Father said, "Nonsense! Pull them out." The dentist said it was a shame to pull the teeth and his shamming nose twisted; but all the time he was looking over my head at my pretty sister who had taken me. He grabbed my head; I clenched my teeth. They bribed me with ten cent pieces and apples till I opened and then I was sorry and bit down on his fingers.

I knew a girl who liked the dentist, but she had only had her teeth filled, never pulled, and he gave her candy. One day she said to me, "I wonder what the dentist's name is? His initials are R.B."

"I know. It is Royal Beast," I said.

Beast was a word we were never allowed to use. I always called the dentist "Royal Beast" after that. It made me feel much better.

"The Snow Storm"

from *The Longest Day of the Year*
by Helen Marquis

Thirteen-year-old Cissy has been left in charge of her younger sister and brother while their parents make Christmas visits in the neighbourhood. Suddenly, a blizzard strikes.

Cissy lifted the lid of the reservoir at the back of the stove and peered in. "No water," she grumbled, and shut it hastily. It was the girls' task to keep the kitchen supplied with water, and they did it week and week-about, alternately. Too often they had complaints from their mother of no water when it was time to do the dishes, or wash all the windows, or scrub the floors. And now Cissy knew just how Mama felt, because Cissy herself had emptied the reservoir doing all the cupboards and had done no refilling. There had been no one here this morning to prod them into remembering. That must be one of the items still unchecked off on their lists. Cissy sighed. Being in the grown-up world with the responsibilities crowding into everything she did wasn't as pleasant as she had thought it would be. It would be nice when Mama was home and she could take over, and Cissy could return to her own world. For a while longer, anyway. She lifted the tea kettle.

It was empty, too.

"I used it all to make the tea," Margie explained hastily.

This was too much.

"Then why didn't you refill it?" Cissy snapped irritably.

"But there was no water in the pails." Margie was reasonable about it.

"In neither?" Cissy didn't believe it was true.

"In neither," Margie echoed.

Still not believing, Cissy looked. Margie was right. The two pails were as dry as a long summer drought. And the pump that was the only source of water for the house stood out in the middle of the yard. In the middle of the storm.

The three stood and looked at one another wordlessly, while the wind outside roared with laughter at their dilemma, and hurled itself at the house, demanding to be let in.

Wearily Cissy started to put on her outdoor clothes. They were still damp from the snow that had blown into the fibres during the last trip outside and had melted there from the warmth of the room. The collar was clammy against her neck.

"You're going to the well?" Tim's voice was squeaking again in his fear. "You'll get lost. And you'll freeze to death. Sure as shooting, you'll get lost."

"I'm going to get snow. To melt. Margie, get me the two pails. My overshoes are still wet enough to make tracks on the floor. And the dishpan, too. Might as well fill that up while I'm at it."

Margie hesitated.

"But Cissy. How'll you fill the things with only one hand? You've got to keep the other on the house."

"I'll try." Cissy felt subtly heroic, and very, very scared. "You two had better get your things on, too. I'll want the lantern on the porch. Tim, do you think you could hold it?"

"Sure. Sure." Tim was getting into the heroic mood, too, struggling into his parka, pulling on boots and cap and wailing that he couldn't find a mitten. Margie found it—Tim had dropped

181

it on the floor and was walking all over it in his search—before bundling into her own things.

But it was no use. All around the house, the wind had blown away the snow to form a runway which Cissy knew without searching stretched several feet out from each wall. The snow had formed that way in lots of smaller storms, she remembered. She staggered back to explain.

Tim came up with one of his preposterous suggestions. "If I held the lantern in the doorway maybe you could see better," he said. Then he added unnecessarily, "I'm thirsty."

Margie hastened to explain the effect of a strong wind on a lighted lantern, which Tim already knew. He was just being exasperating. Cissy cast her eyes upward in a dramatic plea to Heaven to forgive the child such ignorance. Her eyes lit on the rope near the ceiling that stretched across the kitchen, burdened every winter night with the family's outdoor garments so that they could dry during the night for the next day's wearing. Cissy pointed, gibbering in her excitement. "The rope! The rope!"

"What? What?" Tim was puzzled.

Margie looked at Cissy and wondered if she were losing her senses.

"Get the rope down, Margie." And as she climbed up on a chair, Cissy explained. "I'll tie one end on my arm and Margie can hold the other end. Then I can move away from the house without getting lost. I'll keep both hands on the pails and follow the rope back. All Margie has to do is keep the rope tight and pull me in."

Tim burst out with, "Golly, Cissy, you sure are smart."

Cissy forebore to point out that five minutes ago he had been singing a different tune. After all, Tim was only almost-seven. So she kept quiet and allowed him to tie the rope on her arm, and with Margie holding the free end of the rope at the porch door, she started out.

As she unlatched the door, the wind tore it from her grasp and

183

hurled it against the wall. The lantern flared, almost died out; Tim involuntarily stepped back to shelter the flame, and it resumed its burning with only an occasional brighter flicker.

"Keep to the back wall, Tim," Cissy suggested. "The wind won't reach you there to blow out the light. I'll be able to see it straight in front."

Tim moved back.

Before, when fetching the coal, Cissy had had a sense of protection lent by the feel of the rigid wall of the house against her shoulder; every minute she knew exactly where she was, and knew, too, that her return to the shelter and warmth of the kitchen was assured.

But now, once her foot left the last porch step, she was alone in a strange and terrifying world. It was a world flying with blackness that tore at her clothing and sand-papered her face and all but forced her to her knees. Cissy had a terrifying thought that if she ever lost her balance and fell, the gale would hammer her to the earth and hold her there forever. Her mind kept repeating "Go straight out from the house till you come to the snowbank. Straight forward . . . straight . . . straight forward . . ."

She hit the snowbank. Hard.

It was a good thing that she was inching her way instead of breezing along in her usual tempestuous manner. Even at that, she felt as if she'd been rammed against a stone wall. She clapped her hand to her bruised forehead, and the wind, seizing the opportunity, tore one pail from her slackened grasp. It vanished without even a rattle. Mama's good pail! Whatever would she think of her and her carelessness? In her anger at herself, she began to chip away furiously at the snowbank with the rim of the other pail. It refused to be chipped. Foolish Cissy, to imagine that all she had to do was to go out and scoop up a couple of pails of fairly soft snow. Even if it had been soft, it would never, never in this world have stayed in one place long enough to scoop up. This stuff she was trying to break off now was granite, sheer

184

granite rock. If she had been lucky enough to break off any pieces, the wind would probably have carried them away immediately after they were loosened.

A handful of frozen pellets slapped into one cheek and, a minute later, into the other from the opposite direction. Frightened, she wondered if the wind was turning into a cyclone and beginning to turn in circles. Or was she the one who was turning? Panic rose in her throat like sickness and she knew she would never get back. She was lost forever in this furious blackness that was tearing her to shreds. Irrelevantly, she thought of the gift she had received at the school's Christmas party this year, a book on mythology, and the story about the Furies with hearts of stone who lay in wait for lost souls. It must have been on nights like these that the Furies rode about looking for lost souls, and this was the wind of their passing. Another lashing of pellets stung her cheek, and she screamed in sudden terror. "I'm lost—I'm lost." Again the storm took the words from her lips and tossed them into the blackness so precipitously that only her mind heard the words. She wanted to turn and run and run and run. . . . But there was no place to run to, in this wild blind night, and her body was as paralyzed as her mind. She managed a faltering step into the wind.

It was the sudden tug on the rope that brought her out of her terror. Why, she wasn't lost. She was tied to Margie, to the family, to home! How could she have been so silly, standing there and scaring herself half to death. Just because a rather high wind was making things a bit difficult—well, let's face it, very difficult. Difficulter. Difficultest. Cissy giggled weakly. The sound of it in her mind comforted her, but like the other sounds she had made, it was carried away in the gale before it reached even her own ears. It was probably way down south in Dixie by now, she thought, and giggled again. I'm going back, she told herself, feeling another tug on her arm; maybe it's only the wind pulling on the rope, but I'm not doing a thing here. Just getting sillier and sillier. Okay, Tim, Margie, here I come. And hand over hand she guided herself home.

Cissy thumped the pail and its emptiness down indignantly when she stepped back into the shed to be greeted with Tim's "What have you been doing, Cissy? Where's the snow? Why'd you leave the other pail out there? I'm thirsty, Cissy. Awful thirsty."

Cissy ignored him. "Get me the butcher knife, Margie, the one with the long blade."

Tim squeaked. "Why, Cissy? Did you see a wolf out there, Cissy? Don't go again, Cissy!" He was doing a little jig of excitement not unmixed with fear, with the lantern dipping and flaring so that long black oily streaks of soot dirtied the glass.

Margie was waiting for Cissy's reply, but at least she was quiet about it, Cissy noted.

"The banks are so hard I can't chip them," she explained. "So I'm going to cut blocks and carry them in my arms."

Which was how she finally managed. In that country of much snow and low temperatures, all children made snow forts and igloos and block houses in the school yards and their own home yards. That was always part of the winter fun in Saskatchewan. But this certainly was no pleasure, Cissy grumbled to herself, and the wind caught the words again and hurled them away. Out here she had to work in complete darkness, bracing her body against the wind, guiding the knife so that she cut the snowbank and did not lose a few fingers in the process, and then hoisting the block into her arms for the return journey. Here again she was hampered. Not only must she carry the block by clutching it tightly in her arms, but she also had to keep her wrists loose for handling the guiding rope, and keep the knife in one hand. It was slow going but she managed it.

She found both Margie and Tim crying—Margie silently, and Tim in great gusty roars. They were so engrossed in sorrow they didn't see Cissy till she stepped onto the porch. Tim flung himself

187

at her and tried to hug her, snow block and all.

"We thought you were lost, Cissy." Tim gave a final sob.

Cissy put the block down, glad to be relieved of it. "Whoever said snow was light? Not when you have to grope your way along with arms stretched to full capacity around a block about the size of a house!"

Margie, a little ashamed of her baby tears and trying to excuse them, said, "It was awful waiting, Cissy. What kept you?"

What kept her? Didn't they have any—just any idea of what it was like struggling against all of nature single-handed out there? Her answer was short. "I was practising my dance steps. Next time maybe I should telephone back?"

Tim began to shout, "Telephone! Telephone! Cissy—Margie! We haven't phoned Mama in the longest time. I want to phone." He was fairly dancing in his impatience.

"Give Margie the lantern and go do it now." Cissy was glad to get rid of him. Tim, in his eagerness to talk to Mama, almost threw the light at Margie. She had to be quick to catch it. Even at that, she missed the handle and only saved the whole thing from crashing to the floor by grabbing it in her arms. "And don't touch the fires or lamp or—" But the kitchen door slammed on Tim's usual "Bossy!" and the rest of the sentence.

"That's Tim." Margie was exasperated.

"It's a good thing you play on the ball team." Cissy sighed. "Even if it's not the right time to talk, the phone'll keep him busy for a few minutes till we get in there. I'll hurry, now that I know exactly how to do everything. And for goodness sake, don't worry. Nothing'll happen to me."

Once more, Cissy stepped out into the storm.

The gale hit the side of her face like a board. She put up her hand to shield it and nearly stabbed herself with the knife she held. "That's all I need now," she told herself grimly. "A nice wide cut—though I'd never bleed. All my blood's frozen stiff." She plunged on into the darkness. The darkness? It was more than that. It was a blackness full of flying blackness. Her teacher had taught that darkness was just the absence of light. If that were so, then this was an absence of light. If that were so, then this was an absence raised to the nth degree. An absolute absence. A gust stronger than ever tore at her and whipped the rope against her back, sending her body faster than her feet. She staggered, regained her footing, went on, and another gust threw her against the wall of the snowbank. She had arrived.

This time, when she cut the block, she thrust the knife up to the handle in the block itself. Her hands were now free to gather up the rope on her return journey. With her arms full, she turned about, facing the way she had come. Slowly she inched her way along, sliding one foot forward and then the other, gathering the thin cotton rope in through her fingers, the burden in her arms getting heavier by the minute. She paused briefly to shift its weight and in that pause she thought the wind blew less fiercely. The next minute it was tearing at her with renewed fury. She waited, but it did not lessen again. She thought, this is imagination working overtime. Then her fingers reached a knot in the rope.

The knot at the end of the rope? It couldn't be. It wasn't possible. Margie was holding the knot at the end of the rope. She was standing there in the porch with the knot in her hands. To guide her back. To take her safely home, out of the storm. The knot—the knot. . . . There must have been a knot somewhere in its length that she hadn't felt before, that her fingers had slipped past without consciously feeling. She'd have to make sure.

Carefully Cissy lowered the snow block to the ground, clamped it between her ankles against the thrust of the wind, and holding her mitten tip in her teeth, pulled it off her hand. With shaking fingers she felt for the knot, for more rope beyond the knot. Nothing. A terrible empty, chilling nothingness.

For a minute, her paralyzed mind refused to admit the truth, but for only a minute. A harder gust of wind roared at her and sandpapered her face with flying snow. At once she was aware of bare fingers tingling and hurriedly pulled on her mitten. Well, she couldn't just stand here, doing nothing except slowly freezing to death. Slowly? Her chilled fingers answered: it won't take more than a few minutes.

Cissy raised her mittened hands, shielding her face while she considered. Had she shifted directions putting down that block of snow? Turned ever so slightly, pulling in the rope? Which direction was the wind coming from? Still east? It had when she was in the house anyway. It had whammed into the east wall all day, and Aunt Veronica's picture that hung there had been quivering ever since the storm started. So when she stepped out of the house, the wind hit her left cheek. It should be hitting her right cheek now on the return trip. If it hadn't changed. It was hard to judge by the wind outside, though. Near a building it came at a person from every which way. She waited a little longer, testing wind direction with her face. When she thought there was a fiercer gust on the right side, she picked up the snow block and proceeded. It never entered her head to leave the block just lying there. So, with her arms burdened, the knot tucked into her hand, trailing the rope, she shuffled forward, step by cautious step. Once she stopped to feel if the knife was still secure in the snow block, and it was, and she went on. Mama would sure be vexed if Cissy lost that knife. Once she stopped to peer forward, hoping to catch a gleam of lantern light through the storm. There was none. She was alone in a world of cold and snow and howling wind. Doggedly she resumed her slow progress forward.

What had caused this? What series of acts or words led up to this? (Cautious foot forward. Now the other one a little bit farther in front.) Margie was waiting, holding the lantern, thinking she still held the rope end. (Another step and another.) Tim had almost thrown the lantern at her and she'd had to catch it. Which was why she dropped the rope knot. (Again a step. And a step. And a step.) He had thrown the lantern when I said telephone. And she'd said it . . . ''Maybe I should telephone back,'' or something silly like

190

that. (Keep on going.) Because she'd been peeved at him and Margie for crying. For crying because they thought she was lost.

Well, she was lost now, and unexpectedly, she hoped Margie didn't know it, and didn't know she, Margie, had been the one to cause it. Cissy just *had* to get back.

Step by step by step by step by . . . .

Her toes stubbed against an obstacle.

She flapped her free hand from its wrist. Nothing. She dragged her foot up the obstacle. It cleared and was over it, onto a flat surface, stubbing against another obstacle. She stood on it and raised the other foot, placed it beside the first. Then she laughed aloud. She was on the porch steps. And there was the lantern's dim glow, growing brighter.

Cissy said, "Put down the lantern, Margie, and guide me over to the other block so I can pile this on top. I can't see over it."

Margie took her wrist and led her along, and in the shadows she couldn't see that Cissy dropped the knotted rope beside the lantern.

Cissy gratefully flexed her tired arms.

"Will that be enough?" It didn't look much, lying there.

Margie was uncertain, eyeing the blocks. They both knew how little water was contained in even large blocks.

"Maybe I'd better get another," Cissy suggested half-heartedly, hoping Margie would veto the idea, hating to go out again.

But Margie didn't hear the reluctance, only the words. "I really think it would be better, Cissy. Christmas Eve baths, you know."

Cissy took up the knife and turned to her sister. "I'll hurry this time."

"You weren't long that time, Cissy. Though I suppose the awful wind makes it seem longer."

Cissy nodded without speaking.

"Where's the rope? Oh, there." Margie picked it up. "You should tug harder, Cissy. I never felt you at all last time."

"Yeah. Well, give it here, Margie. I'll tie it onto the door handle.

You've got enough to hang onto, keeping the wind from that lantern. Sure helped me come in that time. The light, I mean." Margie beamed as she listened to the praise and watched Cissy tying the rope end securely to the door handle, and tying it once more for good luck.

"Goodness! We'll never get it off now!"

"Then it will be on there for the next storm," Cissy retorted lightly. "Getting cold?"

Margie nodded. Cissy turned to go. "Well, it won't be long this time," she said. "I've got a tunnel through the darkness, but that wind keeps filling it up."

Margie laughed, and the lantern she held close to her stomach bobbled up and down with her laughter. The sound of it followed Cissy out the door until the wind whisked it away.

It took Cissy but a brief while to bring in the third block, and pleased with herself, she went back for another. This time, coming back, she tripped and fell, and broke the block all to pieces, and she had to grope around for the knife. When she found it, she went back for a block to replace that fourth one, and carried it in. But now she was so cold and tired, and her knees hurt where the frozen ground had skinned them in the fall, and Margie was beginning to turn blue. So they called it a day and went in.

The Child's Umbrella
by Raymond Souster

What's it like to be homeless
all alone in this world?

Perhaps the jagged
ripped-open mouth
of the child's umbrella
lying inside out
on the winter pavement

can give us the answer.

"Journal of a Young Girl"

from *A Child in Prison Camp*
by Shizuye Takashima

The distinguished Canadian artist, Miss Takashima, was a child when World War II broke out, and she lived through that unhappy episode in Canadian history when Japanese-Canadians were stripped of their property and sent to internment camps. The following excerpts highlight some of her experiences, and show her sensitive response to nature and people, despite the indignity which her family suffered.

Vancouver, British Columbia
March 1942

Japan is at war with the United States, Great Britain and all the Allied Countries, including Canada, the country of my birth. My parents are Japanese, born in Japan, but they have been Canadian citizens for many, many years, and have become part of this young country. Now, overnight our rights as Canadians are taken away. Mass evacuation for the Japanese!

"All the Japanese," it is carefully explained to me, "whether we were born in Tokyo or in Vancouver are to be moved to distant places. Away from the west coast of British Columbia—for security reasons."

We must all leave, my sister Yuki, my older brother David, my parents, our relatives—all.

The older men are the first to go. The government feels that my father, or his friends, might sabotage the police and their

194

buildings. Imagine! I couldn't believe such stories, but there is my father packing just his clothes in a small suitcase.

Yuki says, "They are going to the foothills of the Rockies, to Tête Jaune. No one's there, and I guess they feel father won't bomb the mountains."

The older people are very frightened. Mother is so upset; so are all her friends. I, being only eleven, seem to be on the outside.

One March day, we go to the station to see father board the train.

At the train station

An empty bottle is tossed in the air.
I stand away, hold my mother's hand.
Angry, dark curses, a scream. A train window is broken.

An angry man is shouting.
The men are dragged violently into the trains.
Father can be seen. He is being pushed onto the train.
He is on the steps, turns. His head is above the
shouting crowd. I see his mouth opening; he shouts
to his friends, waves his clenched fist.
But the words are lost in all the noise.
Mother holds my hand tightly.

A sharp police whistle blows.
My blood stops. We see a uniformed Mounted Police drag
an old man and hurl him into the train.
More curses, threats. The old train bellows
its starting sound. White, hellish smoke appears
from the top of its head. It grunts, gives another
shrill blast. Slowly, slowly, the engine comes to life.
I watch from where we stand, fascinated.
The huge, black, round, ugly wheels begin
to move slowly, then faster, and faster.
Finally, the engine, jet dark,
rears its body and moves with a lurch.

The remaining men rush toward the train,
scramble quickly into the moving machine.

Men crowd at the windows. Father is still on the steps,
he seems to be searching the crowd, finally sees us, waves.
Mother does not move. Yuki and I wave. Most remain still.
The dark, brown faces of the men become small.

Vancouver
September 1942

Now we have curfew. All Japanese have to be indoors by ten P.M.
The war with Japan is fierce. People in the streets look at us with
anger. My sister Yuki has to quit her job. No reason is given by
the elderly lady. We wait, mother, Yuki and I, for our notice to go
to the camps. Already many families have left.

A night out

Yuki holds my hand, begins to run.
"We have to hurry, Shichan. It's close to ten.
Can you run a bit?" "I'll try," I say,
but my limp makes it hard for me to keep up.
Yuki slows down. I wish mother were with us.
Everything seems so dark. An old man comes
towards us, peers at us in the dim light.
His small eyes narrow, he shouts, "Hey, you!
Get off our streets!" He waves his thin arms,
"I'll have the police after you."
Yuki pulls my arm, ignoring him, and we run faster
towards our house. The man screams after us.

Mother is at the door when we arrive.
She looks worried, "You are late." She sees us panting.
"Did you two have trouble?" She closes the door quickly.
"You know I worry when you're late, Yuki."
Yuki sits on a chair, looks at mother.
"I'm sorry. The film was longer than I thought.
It was so great we forgot about the curfew."

Mother pours Japanese green tea. It smells nice.
I sit beside her and drink the hot tea.
I look around. The rooms are bare.
Boxes are piled for storage in the small room upstairs.
Our suitcases are open, they are slowly being filled.
We are leaving for camp next week.

A siren screams in the night. Air-raid practice.
I go to the window. All our blinds are tightly drawn.
I peek out, carefully lifting them. I see
one by one the lights in the city vanish. Heavy
darkness and quiet covers Vancouver. It looks weird.
But the stars, high, high above, still sparkle,
not caring, still beautiful and happy. I feel sad
to be leaving the mountains, the lovely sea.
I have grown with them always near me.

"Come away from the window, Shichran." Mother's voice
reaches me. I turn. I feel sadness come from her too.
She has lived here for so long:
"Over twenty-five years—hard to believe—
I was a young girl, full of dreams.
America! Canada! all sounded so magical in Japan.
Remember, we had no radio in those days, so all our
knowledge of this country came from books.
My own mother had come to Canada long before
other women. She was brave, not knowing the language,
young, adventurous, a widow with three children.
She took your uncle Fujiwara with her.
He was thirteen. I went to my grandmother's;
my sister, to an aunt. It seems so long ago."

Mother often talks of the past. Her life
on the tiny island sounds lovely, for she had
a happy childhood, so full of love.
I go to her. I see her hands folded neatly
on her lap. She always sits like this,
very quiet, calm. Her warm eyes behind her
round glasses are dark and not afraid.

An end to waiting

We have been waiting for months now. The Provincial
Government keeps changing the dates of our evacuation, first from
April, then from June, for different reasons: lack of trains, the
camps are not ready. We are given another final notice. We dare
not believe this is the one.

We rise early, very early, the morning we are to leave.
The city still sleeps. The fresh autumn air feels nice.
We have orders to be at the Exhibition grounds.
The train will leave from there, not from the station
where we said good-bye to father and to David.
We wait for the train in small groups scattered
alongside the track. There is no platform.
It is September 16. School has started. I think
of my school friends and wonder if I shall ever see
them again. The familiar mountains, all purple and
splendid, watch us from afar. The yellowy-orangy
sun slowly appears. We have been standing
for over an hour. The sun's warm rays reach us,
touch a child still sleeping in its
mother's arms, touch a tree, blades of grass.
All seems magical. I study the thin yellow rays
of the sun. I imagine a handsome prince will come and
carry us all away in a shining, gold carriage with
white horses. I daydream, and feel nice as long as I don't
think about leaving this city where I was born.

New Denver, British Columbia
September 1942

Our home at night

It is night. We light our two candles.
There is no electricity.
The frail, rationed candles burst into life and
the darkness slinks away. The smell of fresh-cut trees
burning, fills the room. The pine pitch cracks and pops

in the fire. I sit, watch my mother.
She places the rice pot on the black, heavy stove.

Yuki brings wood. I help her pile it near the
hot stove, for the raw wood is damp.
The family who share the kitchen, the stove and
the house, begin their dinner. Mrs. Kono appears
quietly from her nooklike curtained bedroom,
bows to my mother, washes her rice. The wood sink
gurgles as the water scooped from the lake
plunges quickly down the narrow pipe.
Soon her rice too is cooking on the big,
black stove. The bare, tiny, candle-lit room is
filled with the smell of rice and Japanese food.

The table is set; the white candles create a circle of light on the
wood table. I sit by the flame.
I notice the far corners of the room are dark. This
gives an eerie feeling. Though eyes and mind are getting
used to this kind of light.

I hear Mr. Kono talking to my father. "It's a
blessing our children are healthy and do not mind this.
Imagine eating by candlelight. No water."
Father replies, "We're complaining to the B.C. Security
Commission again. We won't give in. We cannot walk a mile
for drinking water, with the winter coming." Mr. Kono asks,
"Will they listen?" Father's voice is impatient:
"They will have to. After all, it's beyond human dignity."

A strike is called

Tonight father returns home angry.
He tells us this story: "The men who are disabled
or too old to work have been getting twenty-three
dollars a month from the Provincial Government.
They were told from now on they
must pay eleven dollars monthly rent
for their shacks. And yet another outrage.

The Police have closed the houses where the elderly
bachelors and widowers live and locked the doors.
They even took all their food away. Some of
their friends have taken them in.
We've had enough! We are all furious."

Even I am surprised. Goodness, what next?
Father sits silent now. There is a terrible tension
in the air. Suddenly, father stands up, shouts,
"We do not work tomorrow." I jump.
Mother nudges me, a sign to remain silent.
Yuki goes out of the house. I look at mother.
"What do you mean?" she asks.
"We'll go on strike," father announces.
He rises, goes out of the house.

School
October 1942

The strike does not last long. "There is no unity in our community.
Always selfish people, wanting their own gain and this terrible
fear." I hear father speaking to mother. So he and others who had
complained return to work within a few days. Rent is charged to
the elderly and the disabled. The bachelors' house is finally re-
opened. We continue to live with the Konos.

One afternoon the Police come to our house. A big, tall, blond man
asks my father many questions. Father does not give any names,
and quietly says he is not afraid. The Police leave. Mother is very
upset. Father says someone must have reported him to the
R.C.M.P. You can't trust anyone. He is angry. Nothing happens
after the visit, but I think father is often looked at with suspicion,
for he is so outspoken and sharp.

Meanwhile school for us has not begun. I am getting restless. The
Provincial Government of B.C. claims that the Japanese people do
not deserve an education. Yet, my father says, they are taking tax
money for education as well as rent for our houses. Can you
imagine? Every day the elders bravely complain to the B.C.

Security Commission. Finally, during the last week of October, school starts for the children, but just from grades one to eight. "The Japanese people do not need, nor do they deserve, higher education." Father says that's what they told him and Mr. Sumi, our other spokesman. So Yuki cannot finish high school and she has only one more year to go. Mother is very upset. Yuki remains quiet.

We are taught by older girls. They have completed high school, but they are not "teachers," so everything is noisy and very un-school-like at first. We are given correspondence sheets which we must follow. I don't like this at all. We have books, too, but nothing else. I miss the familiar desks and my school friends.

Christmas at home

I swing my legs to and fro. Japanese music
fills our tiny room. Mrs. Kono has a small
record player. From this black, leather box,
with shining handles which we turn from time
to time, glorious music comes. In the hot,
burning oven, our Christmas chicken is cooking.
It sputters and makes funny noises. The lemon pies
father baked are already on the table. He has been
cooking all day. They look so nice,
my favourite pies. Only father can bake
such lovely, tasty pies. He must put magic
into them.

Father is an excellent cook. Before he became a gardener,
he worked as a chef in a big restaurant and in hotels.
And now, he still cooks on holidays or when we have
many guests. I love watching him cook. He never uses
a measuring cup, mostly his hands. He's always tasting,
make gurgling, funny noises in this throat
(for Japanese are allowed to make a lot of noise
when they eat; especially when they drink tea
or eat soup). Father closes his slanted eyes and

203

tastes it, then he gives me a tiny bit. He and mother
always treat me special, I guess because I'm
the youngest and not as strong as Yuki.
She doesn't mind; she knows I love her.
I watch my father cook and I listen.
The old song sounds full of joy . . . .
Father ties a towel around his head. Mother hands
him a bowl. He raises his arm, dances around.
He is graceful as he waves his arm and bowl
in time with the music. We all laugh.
Mr. Kono joins him and sings. It is an old folk song.

The music, our voices, go beyond our house, out
into the snow, past the mountains and into space,
and this special day is made more magic,
 and I know I shall remember it forever.

Father's garden

Father has cleared most of the land around our house. We are in
the wilderness, so this is done with hard work. Every day after
work, he and Mr. Kono clear the trees and stumps. Most of the
Japanese people in Canada are farmers, or gardeners like father. So
they know exactly what to plant and how.

Father is planting seeds. The front of our house
is cleared; the dark, fluffy-looking soil is turned
and hoed. Father says after he plants the seeds here,
 he will finish clearing the land in the back of the house
to plant corn and potatoes and lettuce.
It all sounds nice. Mother says, "This will help
us with the food. You know father makes
very little, only thirty-five cents an hour.
And that is because he's a foreman.
The others make twenty-five cents an hour,
hardly enough to pay for the expensive meat
and vegetables."

Early summer 1943
Water at last!

June arrives, and with it, water! At last, water is piped into the
main streets of the whole camp. It is hard to believe. All spring I
watched the men lay the long, shining pipes, then put in little taps,
one for each eight or nine houses. We still have to go outside to
draw water but now we do not have to walk so far. Our tap is quite
close to our house. It will be especially good for the old people.
They found it so hard to fetch water. Often, the younger boys
brought it for them. Father is pleased. He fought so hard for this.

I look at the pipe with the small, shining tap.
It appears from the ground like a metal snake.
I wonder if it will really work. Slowly, I turn it.
A pause, then the clear water gushes out.
It crashes down into the narrow wood sink
placed flush to the ground. I shout, "It works!" The water
keeps pouring out. Mrs. Kono is standing
with her two buckets. "My," she exclaims, "it's like
a dream. One forgets so quickly that we had water
in our homes at one time. Isn't this wonderful,
Shichan?" We smile at each other with pure happiness.
I touch it with my hands, let it flow through my fingers.

Mother comes with her pot of rice.
"My," she beams, then bends and washes the rice.
Swish, swish, her right hand swirls the wet
rice. It makes a funny, familiar sound.
"We must never again take our water for granted."

Mother looks serious and sighs, straightens herself.
"I heard Mrs. Takeda say they are going to build
a bath-house closeby now that we have water.
Did you hear?" Mrs. Nishimura asks mother. She grins.
"Yes, my husand was talking about it last week.
Then we won't have to walk so far to bathe. A blessing!"

August 1945

We hear the terrifying news. The atomic bomb! Father and mother are silent. Mrs. Kono looks so upset. I go to see Mary. Her mother is crying. There is a terrible tension in the camp. Mr. Mori and the other veterans are openly cursed and threatened. Some blame them for the bomb. No one speaks to Mr. Mori. I saw him this morning. He stared at me. He held his stick very tight to his thin body. I backed away and turned, for I didn't want to pass him. I wondered what he thought as I hurried into the house. I can't understand all this hatred, especially among ourselves. . . .

The end of the war

At last the war with Japan is at an end! We are not surprised, we have been expecting it for months now. It hits the older people very hard. They are given two choices by the Canadian Government: to sign a paper and renounce their Canadian citizenship and return to Japan, or to remain here and be relocated elsewhere. There are terrible quarrels. Those who have signed to return to Japan are called "fools"; the ones who have chosen to stay in Canada are called "dogs", slang for traitors. The Kono family, Mr. Shimizu, our father's friend, all sign to return to Japan. We feel sad that Kay-ko is leaving us. All those families must move to another camp, at Tashme, not far from Vancouver. From there, they will go to Vancouver, then on to Japan.

My mother and I just wait, hoping. Then one day,
out of the blue, father says quietly: "We go east!
I've placed an application. We sign to go to Toronto."
He speaks quietly, more to mother than to me.
"It is useless to return now. My family, God knows
where they are, if any are still alive. I'm glad it's over.
We'll just have to start again. It won't be easy for us."
He looks strange. He rises from his chair quickly
and walks out. I feel sorry for him. The atomic bomb
has upset everyone deeply, too. It seems so wrong.

September 1945

It is almost three years to the day since we left Vancouver. The papers for us to leave for the east come through. This is our last week in New Denver.

I go to the lake for the last time with mother
to rinse our clothes. The water is still warm.
I swish the white sheets in the clear water.
Mother is wringing the clothes. She is singing,
she looks so happy. I wonder what David will
look like. I say, "We won't be doing this in Toronto."
Mother sighs, stops, looks at the mountains.
"All in all, Shichan, the three years have not been very hard,
when you think of all the poor people who have been
killed and hurt, and now the suffering in Japan."

Mother and I look out into the distance. A small bird
swoops gracefully down towards the still water.
Another follows. Their pure joy in doing this
is reflected in their flight. The morning mist is slowly
rising from the lake. It looks like it is on fire.
The sun's rays try to seep through the mist.
Everything looks all misty and grey-yellow. I know
I shall remember this beautiful scene,
doing our chores for the last time with nature
all-giving and so silent. Mother bends her frail body,
continues to rinse the clothes. I go back to helping her.
There is warmth between us, and I feel her happiness.

I try to absorb it all, for I know it will be gone soon.
Toronto is a large city. David has written
it is in flat country, by Lake Ontario.
There are no mountains, no snow-capped mountains.
Instead will be concrete buildings, apartments, buses, cars.
But I am looking forward to this, too. Instead of
the sounds of insects and frogs and wild dogs at night,
we will have street sounds, and go to school with
other children, all kinds of children.

Our last night in camp, I go out of the house.
I watch the red rays of the glorious sun.
It spreads its burning arms to the brilliant early autumn
sky, touches the dark pines in the distance.
They catch fire. I hold my breath.
It is aflame, all red for a long time.

Then the rays of the sun slowly begin to fade
behind the now deep purple mountains. The trees,
the mountains all turn into a dark mysterious silhouette as
I stay rooted to the spot. Night comes on.
The pale, pale moon is suspended in the scarlet sky.
I stay standing a long time watching it,
for I want to remember it forever.

Childhood Summers
by Kim Elkington

I remember the house on the island
we got up early, mornings
and ate lucky charms
on the white veranda for breakfast
and ran
in childish gaiety
to the beach, sand, stone and buried treasure
waters, too wide and too blue.
Our summers
were crickets, at night and
corn
roasting
fire, and the shooting stars that existed for
one second of eternity
midnight. The frogs cried
in the lily pond. We caught tadpoles (polywiggles)
and everything came so easily.
We built forts
in the trees by the pier,
and lived there, as knights and pirates
and buccaneers, and queens
and noble men; we rode the ferries
over silent waters, sliding quietly,
never realizing
that this was a summer,
as only summers could be,
the boardwalk, rotting wood, and a
Rolling Stones song.
the moon set above
us, the sun rose and our
days began again.
The next year we learned
the house
(our house, I thought) had burned down.
At the touch of fire, for someone
else's adventure, our own had died.

Kate's Poem
by Jean Little

When I opened my eyes this morning,
The day belonged to me.
The sky was mine and the sun,
And my feet got up dancing.
The marmalade was mine and the squares of sidewalk
And all the birds in the trees.
So I stood and I considered
Stopping the world right there,
Making today go on and on forever.
But I decided not to.
I let the world spin on and I went to school.
I almost did it, but then, I said to myself,
"Who knows what you might be missing tomorrow?"

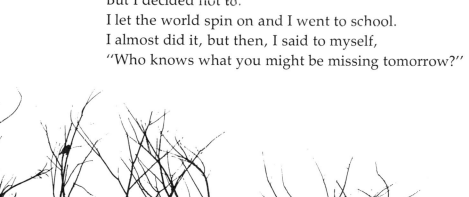

"Saved from the River"

from *The Incredible Journey*
by Sheila Burnford

Three animals, who are being temporarily boarded in northern Ontario, set out on a long journey through the wilderness to their home. On the way they become separated, and the Siamese cat, Tao, nearly drowns.

Many miles downstream on the side to which the dogs had crossed a small cabin stood near the bank of the river, surrounded by three or four acres of cleared land, its solid, uncompromising appearance lightened only by the scarlet geraniums at the window sills and a bright blue door. A log barn stood back from it, and a steam-bath house at the side nearer the river. The patch of vegetable garden, the young orchard and the neatly fenced fields, each with their piles of cleared boulders and stumps, were small orderly miracles of victory won from the dark encroaching forest that surrounded them.

Reino Nurmi and his wife lived here, as sturdy and uncompromising as the cabin they had built with their own hand-hewn logs, their lives as frugal and orderly as the fields they had wrested from the wilderness. They had tamed the bush, and in return it yielded them their food and their scant living from trap lines and a wood lot, but the struggle to keep it in subjection was endless. They had retained their Finnish identity

212

complete when they left their homeland, exchanging only one country's set of solitudes and vast lonely forests for another's, and as yet their only real contact with the new world that lay beyond their property line was through their ten-year-old daughter Helvi, who knew no other homeland. Helvi walked the lonely miles to the waiting school bus each day, and through her they strengthened their roots in the security of the New World, and were content meanwhile with horizons limited by their labour.

On the Sunday afternoon that the beaver dam broke, a day of some relaxation, Helvi was down by the river, skipping flat stones across the water, and wishing that she had a companion; for she found it difficult to be entirely fair in a competition always held against herself. The riverbank was steep and high here, so she was quite safe when a rushing torrent of water, heralded by a great curling wave, swept past. She stood watching it, fascinated by the spectacle, thinking that she must go and tell her father, when her eye was caught by a piece of debris that had been whirling around in a back eddy and was now caught on some boulders at the edge of the bank. She could see what looked like a small, limp body on the surface. She ran along by the boiling water to investigate, scrambling down the bank, to stand looking with pity at the wet, bedraggled body, wondering what it was, for she had never seen anything like it before. She dragged the mass of twigs and branches further up on land, then ran to call her mother.

Mrs. Nurmi was out in the yard by an old wood stove which she still used for boiling the vegetable dyes for her weaving, or peelings and scraps for the hens. She followed Helvi, calling out to her husband to come and see this strange animal washed up by an unfamiliar, swift-surging river.

He came, with his unhurried countryman's walk and quiet thoughtful face, and joined the others to look down in silence at the small limp body, the darkly plastered fur betraying its slightness, the frail skull bones and thin crooked tail mercilessly exposed. Suddenly he bent down and laid his hand lightly on it for a moment, then pulled back the skin above and below one eye and looked more closely. He turned and saw Helvi's anxious, questioning face close to his own, and beyond that her mother's. "Is a drowned *cat* worth trying to save?" he asked them, and when her mother nodded, before Helvi's pleading eyes, he said no more, but scooped the soaking bundle up and walked back to the cabin telling Helvi to run ahead and bring some dry sacks.

He laid the cat down in a sunny patch by the wood stove and rubbed it vigorously with sacking, turning the body from side to side until the fur stood out in every direction and it looked like some dishevelled old scarf. Then, as he wrapped the sacking firmly around and her mother pried the clenched teeth open, Helvi poured a little warm milk and precious brandy down the pale cold throat.

She watched as a spasm ran through the body, followed by a faint cough, then held her breath in sympathy as the cat retched and choked convulsively, a thin dribble of milk appearing at the side of its mouth. Reino laid the straining body over his knee and pressed gently over the ribcage. The cat choked and struggled for breath, until at last a sudden gush of water streamed out, and it lay relaxed. Reino gave a slow smile of satisfaction and handed the bundle of sacking to Helvi, telling her to keep it warm and quiet for a while—if she was sure that she still wanted a cat.

She felt the oven, still warm though the fire had long died out, then placed the cat on a tray inside, leaving the door open. When her mother went into the cabin to prepare supper and Reino left to milk the cow, Helvi sat cross-legged on the ground by the stove, anxiously chewing the end of one fair braid, watching and waiting. Every now and then she would put her hand into the oven to touch the cat, to loosen the sacking or to stroke the soft fur, which was beginning to pulsate with life under her fingers.

After half an hour she was rewarded: the cat opened his eyes.

215

She leaned over and looked closely into them—their blackness now contracted, slowly, to pinpoints, and a pair of astonishingly vivid blue eyes looked up instead. Presently, under her gentle stroking, she felt a throaty vibration, then heard a rusty, feeble purring. Wildly excited, she called to her parents.

Within another half-hour the little Finnish girl held in her lap a sleek, purring, Siamese cat, who had already finished two saucers of milk (which normally he detested, drinking only water), and who had groomed himself from head to foot. By the time the Nurmi family were eating their supper around the scrubbed pine table, he had finished a bowl of chopped meat, and was weaving his way around the table legs, begging in his plaintive, odd voice for more food, his eyes crossed intently, his kinked tail held straight in the air like a banner. Helvi was fascinated by him, and by his gentleness when she picked him up.

That night the Nurmis were having fresh pickerel, cooked in the old-country way with the head still on and surrounded by potatoes. Helvi ladled the head with some broth and potatoes into a saucer and put it on the floor. Soon the fishhead had disappeared to the accompaniment of pleased rumbling growls. The potatoes followed; then, holding down the plate with his paw, the cat polished it clean. Satisfied at last, he stretched superbly, his front paws extended so that he looked like a heraldic lion, then jumped on to Helvi's lap, curled himself around and purred loudly.

The parents' acceptance was completed by his action, though there had never before been a time or place in the economy of their lives for an animal which did not earn its keep, or lived anywhere except the barn or kennel. For the first time in her life Helvi had a pet.

Helvi carried the cat up to bed with her, and he draped himself with familiar ease over her shoulder as she climbed the steep ladder stairs leading up to her little room in the eaves. She tucked him tenderly into an old wooden cradle, and he lay in sleepy contentment, his dark face incongruous against a doll's pillow.

Late in the night she woke to a loud purring in her ear, and felt him treading a circle at her back. The wind blew a gust of cold rain across her face and she leaned over to shut the window, hearing far away, so faint that it died in the second of wind-borne sound, the thin, high keening of a wolf. She shivered as she lay down, then drew the new comforting warmth of the cat closely to her.

When Helvi left in the morning for the long walk and ride to the distant school the cat lay curled on the window sill among the geraniums. He had eaten a large plate of oatmeal, and his coat shone in the sun as he licked it sleepily, his eyes following Mrs. Nurmi as she moved about the cabin. But when she went outside with a bucket of washing she looked back to see him standing on his hind legs peering after, his soundless mouth opening and shutting behind the window. She hurried back, fearful of her geraniums, and opened the door—at which he was already scratching—half expecting him to run. Instead he followed her to the washing line and sat by the basket, purring. He followed her back and forth between the cabin and the wood stove, the henhouse and the stable. When she shut him out once by mistake he wailed pitifully.

This was the pattern of his behaviour all day—he shadowed the Nurmis as they went about their chores, appearing silently on some point of vantage—the seat of the harrow, a sack of potatoes, the manger or the well platform—his eyes on them constantly. Mrs. Nurmi was touched by his apparent need for companionship: that his behaviour was unlike that of any other cat she attributed to his foreign appearance. But her husband was not so easily deceived—he had noticed the unusual intensity in the blue eyes. When a passing raven mocked the cat's voice and he did not look up, then later in the stable sat unheeding to a quick rustle in the straw behind, Reino knew that the cat was deaf.

217

Carrying her schoolbooks and lunch pail, Helvi ran most of the way home across the fields and picked up the cat as well when he came to meet her. He clung to her shoulder, balancing easily, while she performed the routine evening chores that awaited her. Undeterred by his weight she fed the hens, gathered eggs, fetched water, then sat at the table stringing dried mushrooms. When she put him down before supper she saw that her father was right—the pointed ears did not respond to any sound, though she noticed that he started and turned his head at the vibration if she clapped her hands or dropped even a small pebble on the bare floor.

She had brought home two books from the travelling library, and after the supper dishes had been cleared away her parents sat by the stove in the short interval before bed while she read aloud to them, translating as she went. They sat, in their moment of rare relaxation, with the cat stretched out on his back at their feet, and the child's soft voice, flowing through the dark austerity of the cabin, carried them beyond the circle of light from the oil lamp to the warmth and brightness of strange lands . . . .

They heard of seafaring Siamese cats who worked their passages the world over, their small hammocks made and slung by their human messmates, who held them second to none as ship's cats; and of the great proud Siamese Ratting Corps who patrolled the dockyards of Le Havre with unceasing vigilance; they saw, with eyes withdrawn and dreaming, the palace watch-cats of long-ago Siam, walking delicately on thin long simian legs around the fountained courtyards, their softly padding feet polishing the mosaics to a lustred path of centuries. And at last they learned how these nobly born Siamese acquired the kink at the end of their tails and bequeathed it to all their descendants.

And as they listened, they looked down in wonder, for there on the rag rug lay one of these, stretched out flat on his royal back, his illustrious tail twitching idly, and his jewelled eyes on

218

219

their daughter's hand as she turned the pages that spoke of his ancestors—the guardian cats of the Siamese princesses. Each princess, when she came down to bathe in the palace lake, would slip her rings for safe-keeping on the tail of her attendant cat. So zealous in their charge were these proud cats that they bent the last joint sideways for safer custody, and in time the faithful tails became crooked forever, and their children's and their children's children's . . . .

One after another the Nurmis passed their hands admiringly down the tail before them to feel the truth in its bent bony tip; then Helvi gave him a bowl of milk, which he drank with regal condescension before she carried him up the ladder to bed.

That night, and for one more, the cat lay curled peacefully in Helvi's arms, and in the daytime during her absence he followed her parents everywhere. He trailed through the bush after her mother as she searched for late mushrooms, then sat on the cabin steps and patted the dropped corn kernels as she shucked a stack of cobs. He followed Reino and his work horse across the fields to the wood lot and perched on a newly felled pungent stump, his head following their every movement, and he curled by the door of the stable and watched the man mending harness and oiling traps. And in the late afternoons when Helvi returned he was there waiting for her, a rare and beautiful enigma in the certain routine of the day. He was one of them.

But on the fourth night he was restless, shaking his head and pawing his ears, his voice distressed at her back. At last he lay down, purring loudly, and pushed his head into her hand—the fur below his ears was soaking. She saw their sharp black triangles outlined against the little square of window and watched them flicker and quiver in response to every small night sound. Glad for him in his newfound hearing, she fell asleep.

When she woke, later in the night, aware of a lost warmth, she saw him crouched at the open window, looking out over the pale fields and the tall, dark trees below. His long sinuous tail thrashed to and fro as he measured the distance to the ground. Even as her hand moved out impulsively towards him he sprang, landing with a soft thud.

She looked down and saw his head turn for the first time to her voice, his eyes like glowing rubies as they caught the moonlight, then turn away—and with sudden desolation she knew that he had no further need of her. Through a blur of tears, she watched him go, stealing like a wraith in the night towards the river that had brought him. Soon the low swiftly running form was lost among the shadows.

Going Up North
by Dennis Lee

I'm going up north and live in the bush
Cause I can't stand parents that nag and push!

I'm going up north and live in a shack,
So tell my parents that I'm never coming back!
And I won't write letters,
    But I think I'll take a snack.

I'm going up north and I'll see strange sights.
I'll be all on my own with the Northern Lights.
I shall whistle to myself
    When the grizzly bears prowl,
And they'll say to one another
    As they snuffle and growl,
"I think I hear a tea kettle
    Coming to the boil,
Or maybe it's a radio
    That's going for a stroll,
Or an operatic porcupine
    Practising a role;
Imagine that—a porcupine
    Practising a role!"
Then the bears will start to fidget
    As they're lolloping along,
Cause a porcupine's ferocious
    If you interrupt his song;
And they'll mutter back and forth,
    "This is not the place for me—
I don't *want* to eat a porcupine—
    I think it's time to flee!"
And I'll squeak a sort of YES!
    And I'll maybe whistle less
And they'll never even guess
    That it's me.

Then I'll sneak back home in the dark of night
And I'll see my parents taking fits with fright
And I won't say Sorry.
   Or, Glad to be back,
But I'll give them a squeeze
   And quickly remark,
"What *marvellous* weather
   We're having today!

Did anything happen
   While I was away?
The grizzlies were great;
   And oh, by the way,
I hope you'll be nicer
   than yesterday."

A Man

by Ernest Buckler

Call the man Joseph. Call his son Mark. Two scars had bracketed Mark's left eye since he was twelve. But they were periods, not brackets, in the punctuation of his life. The reason had to do with his father.

Joseph had none of the stiffness that goes with rock strength. He was one of those men who cast the broadest shadow, without there being any darkness in them at all. Yet there was always a curious awkwardness between him and his son. In a neighbour's house of a Sunday afternoon Mark might stand nearer to him than to anyone else; but he never got onto his lap like the other kids got onto their fathers' laps. Joseph never teased him. He never made him any of those small-scale replicas of farm gear that the other men made their sons: tiny ox carts or trail sleds.

In any case, that kind of fussy workmanship was not his province. His instrument was the plow.

One day he came across Mark poking seeds between the potato plants.

"What's them?" he said.

Mark could dodge anyone else's questions; he could never answer his father with less than the whole truth.

"They're orange seeds," he said.

He'd saved them from the Christmas before. Oranges were such a seldom thing then that it was as if he was planting a mystery.

"They won't grow here," Joseph said.

Mark felt suddenly ridiculous, as he so often did when his father came upon anything fanciful he was doing: as if he had to shift himself to the sober footing of common sense. He dug the seeds out and planted them, secretly, behind the barn.

The night of the accident was one of those cold, drizzly nights in early summer when animals in the pasture huddle like forlorn statutes. The sort of night when the cows never come.

School had ended that very day. This was the third year Mark had graded twice and he was very excited. All the time his mother washed the supper dishes he kept prattling on about the kings and queens of England he'd have in his studies next term. He felt two feet taller than the "kid" he'd been yesterday.

His father took no part in the conversation, but he was not for that reason outside it—and everything Mark said was for his benefit too.

Joseph was waiting to milk. "Ain't it about time you got after the cows?" he said at last. He never ordered Mark. It would have caused the strangest sort of embarrassment if he ever had.

Cows! Mark winced. Right when he could almost *see* the boy Plantagenet robed in ermine and wearing the jewelled crown!

"They'll come, won't they?" he said. (He knew better.) "They come last night."

He never used good speech when his father was around. He'd have felt like a girl. (Though Joseph was a far wiser, far better educated man in the true sense than Mark would ever be.)

"They won't come a night like this," Joseph said. "They're likely holed up in a spruce thicket somewheres, outa the rain."

"I'll see if I can hear the bell," Mark said.

He went out on the porch steps and listened. There wasn't a sound.

"It's no use to wait for the bell," Joseph called. "They won't budge a hair tonight."

"Well, if they ain't got sense enough to come themselves a night like this," Mark said, as near as he'd ever come to sputtering at his father, "why can't they just stay out?"

"I'd never get em back to their milk for a week," Joseph said.

Mark went then, but, as Joseph couldn't help seeing, grudgingly.

He sat on the bars of the pasture gate and called. "*Co*-boss, *co*-boss. . . ." But there wasn't the tinkle of a bell.

He loved to be out in a good honest rain, but this was different. He picked his steps down the pasture lane to avoid the clammy drops that showered from every bush or fern he touched.

He came to the first clearing, where Joseph had planted the burntland potatoes last year. The cows were nowhere to be seen. But Pedro, the horse, was there—hunched up and gloomy-looking in the drizzle. Mark couldn't bear to see him so downcast and not try to soothe him.

He went close and patted his rump. Pedro moved just far enough ahead to shake off his touch. It was the kind of night when the touch of anything sent a shivery feeling all through you.

He should have known that the horse wanted to be left alone. But he kept at it. He'd touch him, the horse would move ahead, he'd follow behind and touch him again. The horse laid back his ears.

And then, in a flash, Mark saw the big black haunch rear up and the hoof, like a sudden devouring jaw, right in front of his left eye. The horse wasn't shod or Mark would have been killed.

He was stunned. But in a minute he got to his feet again. He put his hand to his face. It came away all blood. He began to scream and run for home.

Joseph could hear him crying before he came in sight. He started to meet him. When Mark came through the alder thicket below the barn and Joseph saw he was holding his hand up to his face, he broke into a run. Before he got to the bars he could see the blood.

He didn't stop to let down a single bar. He leapt them. Mark had never seen him move like that in his life before. He grabbed Mark up and raced back to the house.

Within minutes the house was a hubbub of neighbours. Mark gloried in the breathless attention that everyone bent on him. He asked Joseph to hold him up to the mirror over the sink. "No, no, Joseph, don't . . . ." his mother pleaded, but Joseph obeyed him.

His face was a mass of cuts and bruises. He felt like a Plantagenet borne off the field with royal wounds.

Afterward, he remembered all the head-shakings: "That biggest cut there don't look too good to me. Pretty deep . . . ."

And the offers of help: "I got some b'racit acit for washin out cuts, down home. I could git it in a minute . . . ."

And the warnings: "No, *don't* let him lay down. Anyone's had a blow on the head, always keep em moving around . . . ."

And he remembered his mother beseeching him over and over: "Can you see all right? Are you sure you can see all right?"

He didn't remember his father doing or saying anything flustered, unusual. But Joseph would be the one who'd quietly put the extra leaves in the dining-room table so they could lay him on it when the doctor came at last, to have the stitches taken. And when the doctor put him to sleep (though he confessed that this was risky, with Mark's weak heart) it would be Joseph's hand that held the chloroform cone without a tremor.

The doctor said that Mark must stay in bed for two whole weeks. Joseph came in to see him once each day and again just before bedtime. Mark's eye was now swollen shut and the colour of thunder sunsets. Maybe he'd have the mirror in his hand, admiring his eye, when he heard his father coming. He'd thrust the mirror in under the bedclothes. They exchanged the same awkward sentences each time. Joseph was the sort of man who looks helplessly out of place in a bedroom. He never sat down.

The first morning Mark was allowed outdoors again he had planned to walk; but Joseph picked him up without a word and carried him.

He didn't protest. But this time there was no tumult of excitement as before to leave him mindless of his father's arms about him; now the unaccustomed feel of them seemed to make him aware of every ounce of his own weight. And yet, though it was merely an ordinary fine summer's morning, it struck him as the freshest, greenest, sunniest he had ever seen.

The moment they left the house it was plain to him that this wasn't just an aimless jaunt. His father was taking him somewhere.

Joseph carried him straight across the house field and down the slope beyond—to where he'd stuck the orange seeds in the ground.

Mark saw what they were headed for before they got there. But he couldn't speak. If he had tried to, he'd have cried.

Joseph set him down beside a miniature garden.

Miniature, but with the rows as perfectly in line as washboard ribs. This had been no rough job for the plow. It had been the painstaking work of fork and spade and then the careful moulding by his hands. He must have started it right after the accident, because the seeds were already through the ground. And he hadn't mentioned it to a soul.

"This can be yours," he said to Mark.

"Oh, Father," Mark began, "it's . . . ." But how could he tell him what it was? He bent down to examine the sprouts. "What's them?" he said, touching the strange plants in the outside row.

"Melons," Joseph said, pointing, "and red peppers and citron."

He must have got them from the wealthy man who had the big glass hothouse in town. Things almost as fanciful as orange seeds.

"You never know," he said. "They might grow here."

Mark could not speak. But his face must have shown the bright amazement that raced behind it, or else what Joseph said next would never have broken out.

"You don't think I'da made you go for them cows if I'd a knowed you was gonna get hurt, do you?" he said. Almost savagely. "I wouldn'ta cared if they'd a never give another drop o' milk as long as they lived!"

Mark gave him a crazy answer, but it didn't seem crazy to either of them then, because of a sudden something that seemed to bridge all the gaps of speech.

"You jumped right over the bars when you saw I was hurt, didn't you!" he said. "You never even took the top one down. You just jumped right clear over em!"

His father turned his face away, and it looked as if his shoulders were taking a long deep breath.

Joseph let him walk back to the house.

When they went into the kitchen, Mark's sister said, "Where did you go?"

For no reason he could explain Mark felt another sudden compact with his father, that this should be some sort of secret.

"Just out," he said.

"Just out around," Joseph echoed.

And Mark knew that never again would he have to . . . shift . . . himself at the sound of his father's footsteps. Not ever.

Drums of My Father
by Shirley Daniels

A hundred thousand years have passed
Yet, I hear the distant beat of my father's drums.
I hear his drums throughout the land,
His beat I feel within my heart.

The drums shall beat, so my heart shall beat,
And I shall live a hundred thousand years.

Information about the Authors

Hazel Boswell
Hazel Boswell was born in Quebec City, and spent most of her summers
on her grandfather's seigneury, where she heard many French-
Canadian legends. She has travelled widely in Canada and Europe,
studying the watercolour techniques which she uses to illustrate her
stories.

Ernest Buckler
Ernest Buckler was born in 1908 in Dalhousie West, Nova Scotia, and
he has lived on the family farm ever since except for a brief period in
Toronto. His novel for adults, *The Mountain and the Valley* (1952), is
considered a Canadian classic.

Sheila Burnford
Sheila Burnford was born in 1918 in Scotland. In 1951 she came to
Canada and settled in Ontario. Her best-known work, *The Incredible
Journey*, has been made into a Walt Disney film and has been translated
into at least twenty-five languages. She has written articles, poems,
stories, and essays, and has won many awards for her writing.

Natalie Carlson
Natalie Carlson is an American who was born in Virginia, and has lived
in Maryland, the Pacific Northwest, Oklahoma, and Honolulu, where
she was at the time of the Pearl Harbor attack. The story in this
anthology is a skillful retelling of a group of stories handed down
through her mother from her French-Canadian great-great-uncle,
Michel Meloche.

Emily Carr

Emily Carr (1871-1945) was born in Victoria, British Columbia, and studied art in San Francisco and England. She is best known for her paintings of Indian life and of the British Columbia forests, but her writing is also lively and colourful. Her first book, *Klee Wyck* (1941) won the Governor General's Award. *The Book of Small* (1942) is made up of reminiscences of her childhood.

George Clutesi

George Clutesi is a West Coast Indian of the Tse-Shaht tribe, a branch of the Nootkas, and was born, raised, and educated on the Reserve near Port Alberni, British Columbia. Clutesi was an intimate friend of the late Emily Carr, who inspired him to paint and write. He was commissioned to paint a large Indian mural in the Canadian Pavilion at Expo '67. In 1970 Clutesi was writer-in-residence at the University of British Columbia and lectured in a cross-cultural education course. The following year he received an honorary doctorate from U.B.C. He is well known for his two books, *Son of Raven, Son of Deer* and *Potlatch,* and he is in frequent demand as a lecturer.

Barbara Cormack

Barbara Cormack was born in 1903 in Manchester, England. Emigrating to Canada in 1940, she settled in Alberta, where she taught school for many years. She has written poetry as well as several adult and juvenile novels. *Westward Ho! 1903,* a tale of the prairie settlement, shows her interest in Western history.

Edward Field

The translator of two of the Eskimo poems in this collection, *The Giant Bear* and *Heaven and Hell,* Edward Field was born in Brooklyn, New York, in 1924. As a child, he played cello in the Field Family Trio (with his two sisters) and had a weekly radio programme on a local station while in high school. He was a navigator in World War II, and has worked as a machinist, farmer, warehouse worker, actor and typist. He now lives in New York City, giving poetry readings and workshops. He has published *Stand Up, Friend, With Me* (Grove, 1963), *Variety Photoplays* (Grove, 1967), *Eskimo Songs and Stories* (Delacorte, 1973), and has won the Lamont Award, the Shelly Memorial Award and the Guggenheim Fellowship. He wrote the narration for the documentary film *To Be Alive,* which played at the New York and Montreal World Film Fairs and won an Academy Award.

Grey Owl

George Stansfeld Belaney (1888-1938) was born in Hastings, England, and emigrated to Canada in 1903. He became a guide and trapper in

Northern Ontario, married an Indian woman, and took the pseudonym of "Grey Owl", claiming that he was Indian. After service in World War I, he returned to northern Quebec and then moved to Alberta, giving up the trapper's life for that of a conservationist, particularly of beaver. He wrote five books about the northern forests, and with these and his lecture tours, he aroused much public interest in conservation. *The Adventures of Sajo and Her Beaver People* (1935) was written for his daughter Dawn.

Roderick Haig-Brown

Roderick Haig-Brown, born in England in 1908, is a naturalist, historian, and an internationally known novelist. He is author of over twenty books, fiction and non-fiction, including many intended for juvenile readers. He won the "Children's Book of the Year" medals for *Starbuck Valley Winter* and *The Whale People,* and he received the Governor-General's Award for *Saltwater Summer.* Educated in England, Roderick Haig-Brown came to Canada at age eighteen and worked in western logging camps. Eventually he married and settled in his present home, Campbell River, British Columbia, where he has served many years as a magistrate.

Kay Hill

Kay Hill is a Nova Scotian, and lives in a village near the mouth of Halifax Harbour. She is a writer of many plays for radio and television, and has adapted the legends of the Wabanaki for C.B.C. television. Her adaptations are offered in book form in *Glooscap and His Magic* (1963), *Badger, the Mischief Maker* (1965), and *More Glooscap Stories* (1970). Her novel *And Tomorrow the Stars: The Story of John Cabot* won the 1968 medal for the Best Children's Book in English, awarded by the Canadian Association of Children's Librarians, and 1971 she won the Vicky Metcalf Award for "a body of work inspirational to Canadian youth".

James Houston

James Houston is a Toronto-born artist now based in New York City, where he is a writer and sculptor in glass. He is associate Director of Design for Steuben Glass, and has won awards for *Takta'liktak* (1965) and *The White Archer* (1967), two children's books which he has written and illustrated. As an artist, Houston's interest was originally directed to primitive cultures and to Eskimo art in particular. He recognized the Eskimo genius for carving on his first journey to the Canadian Arctic in 1948, and he set to work to bring it to the attention of the outside world. In addition, he introduced the art of printmaking to the Eskimo, based on their traditional technique of incised drawings on stone and bone. James Houston brings to the art of writing the beauty of simplicity and poetic feeling that exist in his sculpture and his drawings.

Archibald Lampman

Archibald Lampman (1861-1899) was born in Morpeth, Canada West, and was educated at Trinity College, Toronto. He spent most of his short life as a civil servant in Ottawa, and from 1888 onwards wrote five volumes of verse, two of which were published posthumously. They were edited by Lampman's friend and fellow-poet, Duncan Campbell Scott, who also prepared Lampman's *Poems* (1900) and *Selected Poems* (1947). Lampman's chief passion was the Canadian countryside, particularly that of Ontario and Quebec, which he described in colourful detail in his verse.

Dennis Lee

At age thirty-five Dennis Lee is considered one of Canada's major poets. In 1972 he won the Governor General's Award for *Civil Elegies* (1968, rewritten 1972). He has taught university, edited books, served as Chairman of Canada Council's advisory arts panel, and he is a political, cultural, and social critic. He lives in Toronto with his family. His best-known book of children's poems, *Alligator Pie*, reflects a distinctively Canadian sense of place, an unusual playfulness with words and rhythms, and a unique sense of humour which appeals to children. He is in great demand for his poetry readings.

Jean Little

Jean Little is an internationally-translated author of many excellent children's novels — *Mine For Keeps, From Anna, Look Through My Window, Kate, Spring Begins in March, Home From Far, One to Grow On, Take Wing,* and others — and has received various awards, including the Vicky Metcalf Award. Jean Little was born in Taiwan where her parents were serving as medical doctors, but the war forced them to return to Guelph, Ontario, her primary residence since childhood. She received a BA degree in English Language and Literature from the University of Toronto. She has travelled widely in Russia and Europe, taught in the United States and Canada, and has lived two years in Japan. She is frequently called upon as a lecturer, and she continues to write for children.

Cyrus Macmillan

Cyrus Macmillan (1882-1953) was born in Wood Islands, Prince Edward Island and was educated at McGill University and at Harvard. He served in World War I, taught at McGill, and held various government posts during his career. He was author of a history of McGill University and of several volumes of Canadian folk music and tales, one of the most famous of which was *Glooscap's Country*, reissued recently under its original title *Canada Wonder Tales*.

Lorrie McLaughlin
Lorrie McLaughlin, a free-lance writer since 1950, is the author of many articles, short stories, and radio-scripts published and broadcast in Canada and the United States.

Helen Marquis
Helen Marquis was born in Sarnia, Ontario, and moved to Saskatchewan when her father took up a homestead there. After working her way through college, she taught school, and her interest in young people has continued with work as a 4-H counselor and as a director at a Farm Camp for girls. The parents of four children, she and her husband actively work a large farm near the area where the story in this book takes place. The storm she writes of was a real one, a blizzard which occurred in 1959.

Ronald Melzack
Ronald Melzack is an eminent, internationally-known psychologist who has been writing children's stories for more than twenty years. Born and educated in Montreal, Melzack has held various academic appointments, and he is now a professor of psychology at McGill. Many of his scientific writings appear in standard psychology texts and journals. Another of his books for children, *The Day Tuk Became a Hunter* (1967), reflects his interest in Eskimo folklore.

Maurice Metayer
Father Maurice Metayer, a member of the Oblate Order, has served in the Canadian Arctic since 1939, and presently lives in Cambridge Bay. Born in St. Malo, France, Father Metayer is the author of numerous books and articles on Eskimo mythology and linguistics, among them *Arlock l'Eskimau, Tradition Esquimaude,* and *I, Nuligak.*

L. M. Montgomery
Lucy Maude Montgomery (1874-1942) was born in Clifton, Prince Edward Island and was educated at Prince of Wales College, Charlottetown, and at Dalhousie University. She worked as a newspaper reporter and as a teacher before marrying the Rev. Ewen MacDonald in 1911 and moving to Norval, Ontario. Of her many children's novels and short stories, the two series beginning with *Anne of Green Gables* (1908) and *Emily of Silver Moon* (1923) are the best known. Her first book in the Anne series, *Anne of Green Gables,* has been translated into many languages, as well as being made into two movies. She was awarded the O.B.E. in 1935.

Susanna Moodie
Susanna Moodie (1803-1885), a sister of Catherine Parr Trail and Samuel Strickland, was born in Suffolk, England, and she and her husband,

J. W. D. Moodie, emigrated to Upper Canada in 1832. Their struggle to adjust to life in the backwoods of Cobourg and Douro township is described in *Roughing It in the Bush* (1952), while their later settlement in the new town of Belleville supplied the material for *Life in the Clearings* (1853). Mrs. Moodie also contributed frequently to the *Literary Garland* and became an editor of the *Victoria Magazine*. She died in Toronto in 1885.

Sir Charles G. D. Roberts

Sir Charles G. D. Roberts (1860-1945) was born in Douglas, New Brunswick, and was educated at the University of New Brunswick. He was a prolific poet, fiction writer and editor. The first of the Confederation poets, he produced nearly twenty volumes of verse, in which the best-known poems are those describing the Maritime landscape and the annual round of rural life. He also published many collections of short stories, most of which were about animals and adventure out of doors. He was elected to the Royal Society of Canada in 1890, and was awarded the Lorne Pierce Medal for distinguished service to Canadian literature in 1926. He was knighted in 1935. His widow, Lady Joan Roberts, is living in Central America.

Robert Service

Robert Service (1874-1958) was born in Preston, England, and was educated in Glasgow. In 1894 he emigrated to British Columbia, and later moved to the Yukon, where by 1908 his verse was bringing in sufficient royalties to enable him to retire. His best-known collection of ballads is *Songs of a Sourdough* (1907), but he also produced sixteen other books of verse, and five melodramatic novels.

Ernest Thompson Seton

Ernest Thompson (1860-1946), who later added the name Seton, was born in South Shields, England, and came to Canada West in 1866, where he was educated at the Ontario College of Art. During a roving life as an artist and naturalist he wrote and illustrated about forty books of animal and woodcraft stories, as well as producing three scholarly works on birds and mammals. Most of his later life was spent in the United States, where he founded the Woodcraft League, became chief of the Boy Scouts of America, and established the Seton Institute at Santa Fe, New Mexico.

Raymond Souster

Raymond Souster was born (1921) and educated in Toronto, and has edited several poetry magazines, as well as writing eleven books of verse. He is chiefly known as a poet of Toronto who accepts and enjoys urban life, though his poems range widely over other places and subjects.

Shizuye Takashima
Shizuye Takashima is a Canadian artist whose paintings are in Canada's leading museums and major private collections. Just emerging from an invalid childhood in 1941, she was among the 22,000 men, women, and children of Japanese origin who were stripped of civil rights and often property. Takashima recreates her three years in a Japanese internment camp through both words and watercolour paintings in her *A Child in Prison Camp* (Tundra, 1971). Miss Takashima now lives in Toronto.

Note
Information was not available about the following authors: Shirley Daniels, Frances Fraser, Kaikshuk, M. Panegoosho, W. Percival Way. Joanne Lysyk and Kim Elkington are students.

The Editors
Mary Rubio and Glenys Stow teach in the Department of English at the University of Guelph and are Associate Editors of the journal *Canadian Children's Literature*.

The Consultant
Ken Haycock is Educational Media Consultant for the Wellington County Board of Education and President of the Executive Council of the periodical *Canadian Materials*, published by the Canadian School Librarians' Association.

Credits

241

George Clutesi: "How the Human People Got the First Fire" from *Son of Raven, Son of Deer* (1967), reprinted with permission of Gray's Publishing Limited, Sidney, B. C.

Barbara Cormack: "The Berry Patch" from *Westward Ho! 1903* (1967), reprinted with permission of Burns and MacEachern Limited.

Shirley Daniels: "Drums of My Father" from *I Am an Indian* (Dent and Sons [Canada] Limited, 1969), reprinted with permission of the author.

Kim Elkington: "Childhood Summers" from *Poetry 73,* reprinted with permission of the Toronto Board of Education.

Edward Field: "The Giant Bear" and "Heaven and Hell" from *Songs and Stories of the Netsilik Eskimo,* part of the upper elementary school course *Man: A Course of Study* developed by the social studies programme of EDC under a grant from the National Science Foundation. Text ©1967, 1968, used with permission of the Education Development Center, Inc.

Frances Fraser: "The Girl Who Married the Morning Star" from *The Bear Who Stole the Chinook* (1959), reprinted with permission of The Macmillan Company of Canada.

Grey Owl: "The Little Prisoner" from *Sajo and Her Beaver People* (1936), reprinted with permission of The Macmillan Company of Canada, Peter Davies, Limited of London, and Charles Scribner's Sons.

Roderick Haig-Brown: "Panther Cubs" from *Panther* (1934), reprinted with permission of Collins Publishers, Toronto, and Houghton Mifflin Company.

Kay Hill: "The Rabbit Makes a Match" from *More Glooscap Stories* (1970), ©1970 by Kay Hill, reprinted with permission of McClelland and Stewart Limited, Dodd, Mead and Company, Inc., and Collins-Knowlton-Wing, Inc.

James Houston: "Across the Mountains" from *Akavak* (1968), ©1968 by James Houston, reprinted with permission of Longman Canada Limited, and Harcourt Brace Jovanovich, Inc.

Dennis Lee: "Going Up North" from *Nicholas Knock and Other People* (1974), reprinted with permission of The Macmillan Company of Canada Limited.

Joanne Lysyk: "The North Wind" from *Pandora's Box,* a classroom kit of 100 poster-poems submitted in a national student poetry contest, sponsored by the Canadian Council of Teachers of English, reprinted with permission of CCTE, English Dept., Glendon College, 2275 Bayview Avenue, Toronto.

Jean Little: "Kate's Poem" from *Look Through My Window* (1970), ©1970 by Jean Little, reprinted with permission of Harper and Row, Publishers, Inc.

Cyrus Macmillan: "The Boy in the Land of the Shadows" from *Canadian Wonder Tales* (reprinted 1974), reprinted with permission of The Bodley Head.

Lorrie McLaughlin: "How the Main John Got His Name" from *Shogomoc Sam* (1970), reprinted with permission of The Macmillan Company of Canada Limited.

Helen Marquis: "The Snow Storm" from *The Longest Day of the Year* (1969), ©1969 Helen Marquis, reprinted with permission of Hawthorn Books, Inc.

Ronald Melzack: "How Raven Created the World" from *Raven, Creator of the World* (McClelland & Stewart, 1970), ©by Ronald Melzack, reprinted with permission of McClelland and Stewart Limited, Weiser & Feeley of New York, and Little, Brown and Company.

Maurice Metayer: "Kajortoq and the Crow" from *Tales from the Igloo* (1972), reprinted with permission of Hurtig Publications.

L. M. Montgomery: "Vanity and Vexation of Spirit" from *Anne of Green Gables* (1908), reprinted with permission of Farrar, Straus, and Giroux, Inc.

Susanna Moodie: "The Fire" slightly adapted from *Roughing It in the Bush* (1852, renewal, 1970), reprinted with permission of McClelland and Stewart Limited.

Sir Charles G. D. Roberts: "The Bear Who Thought He Was a Dog" from *Thirteen Bears* (1947), reprinted with permission of Lady Roberts.

Robert Service: "The Cremation of Sam McGee" from *The Collected Poems of Robert Service* and *Songs of a Sourdough* (Ryerson, 1969), reprinted with permission of McGraw-Hill Ryerson Limited, Dodd, Mead and Company, Inc., and Ernest Benn of London.

Ernest Thompson Seton: "Silverspot" from *Wild Animals I Have Known* (1899) reprinted with permission of Anya Seton Chase.

Raymond Souster: "The Child's Umbrella" from *The Colour of the Times/Ten Elephants on Yonge Street*, reprinted with permission of McGraw-Hill Ryerson Limited.

Shizuye Takashima: selection "Journal of a Young Girl" taken from *A Child in Prison Camp*, ©Shizuye Takashima 1971, Tundra Books Inc. Montreal.

Design and Cover:
Michael van Elsen

Illustrations and Photographs:
Kim Attwell, Grade 5, 223
Alec Burns, Photo Source, 67
George W. Calef, 14-15
Lissa Calvert, 19, 75, 83, 89, 94, 135, 143, 149, 178
Clive Dobson, 183, 187, 215, 219, 227
K. F. Dudley, 126
Roger Duvoisin, 107, 113, from *The Talking Cat and Other Stories of French
    Canada* by Natalie Savage Carlson. Copyright, 1952, by Natalie Savage
    Carlson. Reprinted by permission of Harper & Row, Publishers, Inc.
Laszlo Gal, 39, 43, 55, 57, 99, 103
Margarete Kaufhold, 26, 31, 33
Miller Services, 174
Ontario Ministry of Natural Resources, 12
Lypa Pitsiulak, "Agakook", Pangnirtung Innuit Co-operative, 25
Public Archives of Canada, 3, 6-7, 10-11, 47, 70, 116, 198-199, 204
Qarliksag, "Eskimo Gymnastic Games", Canadian Arctic Producers
    Limited, 50
Doug Schave, Grade 5, 156-157
Christine Stahle, Grade 5, 158
Jimmy Stewart, Grade 5, 160
Michael van Elsen, 193, 211
    The publisher and editors were unable to locate the copyright holder of
        the etching on page 63. Any information regarding this illustration
        would be appreciated.

Pilot programme:
Ken Haycock, Anne Crocker, Linda Braine, Virginia Davis, Jean
    Guerriero, Murray Heslop, Nancy Horgan, Isla Key, Maureen
    Pammett, Don Rahrick, Sandra Shepherd, Joan Skelton, Jean Stevens,
    Joyce Watson, Helen Wilson, Ruth Wright.